What People Say About *Lorraine B. Kingdon* as a Speaker, Teacher and Writer:

"You continue to perform your work as a communicator and news editor at the highest level...You're regarded as one of the top news writers in your profession." Patricia Calvert, Deputy Director, Communication, Information and Technology, U.S. Department of Agriculture, Washington, DC

"Thank you for your presentation at the first CENTRL environmental issues seminar. I believe each participant now has a much better understanding of the media and how best to deal with those in the media regarding environmental issues." Jim P.M. Chamie, Ph.D., CENTRL Executive Director, Phoenix, AZ

"Your media workshops became the focus of a new direction for rural interests and have galvanized action...Ranching and land management interests have realized they can and must present their story to the public. Thank you." Eric Schwennesen, Cooperative Extension, University of Arizona, Tucson, AZ

Take the Mystery Out Of Media

Make Your Publicity Newsworthy

Lorraine B. Kingdon

COMMUNICATION SKILLS INSTITUTE

This publication is designed to provide accurate and authoritative information concerning the subject matter covered. It is sold with the understanding that neither the author nor the publisher are engaged in rendering legal or other professional services.

Jeff Neff, Cover and Design

Kingdon, Lorraine B.
Take the Mystery Out Of Media: Make Your Publicity Newsworthy
ISBN 0-9640861-0-7 (pbk)
1. Publicity   2. Media

CIP 94-71492

All inquiries should be addressed to:
Communication Skills Institute
1821 N. Camino Sabadell
Tucson, AZ 85715

CONTENTS

Why Deal With Media?

It's quite simple. You need to deal with media because your customers...the people you must reach in your business, whoever they are...pay attention to what they read, listen to, or watch.

In a 1991 study, Cornell University communication researchers Yarborough and Scherer discovered:

- 84 percent of Americans watch television every day;
- 75 percent read a newspaper at least 45 minutes every day;
- 75 percent listen to the radio;
- 94 percent read at least one magazine every month;
- 50 percent read one book a month.

These statistics may surprise you. The point is: you take a high risk ignoring media. All those customers you want to reach are paying attention to what they read, and hear, and see.

▪ Media can give you credibility...or destroy it.

▪ Media can endorse your products or services to large numbers of possible customers...or they can label you a fraud.

▪ Media can take your message, speedily and efficiently, to audiences you want to reach...but you have little control over **when** that message is delivered or **how** it is phrased.

In this book, I deal with news and publicity, not with advertising. You *buy* advertising; you *control* exactly where and when it appears, what it says and how it looks. You gain publicity through news departments; you can't control its appearance.

Media rules are made by professionals: the journalists.

News is the business of the media; they're the professionals, and they determine news coverage. The fact that you may be an advertiser gives you little, if any, voice in handling news. It's true; your advertising helps pay the bills and make the newspapers, magazines or television and radio stations profitable. But the news operation and the advertising department are separate entities.

Your advertising dollars won't keep your disastrous fire (or the possibility it was caused by arson) out of the paper no matter how much you plead. On the other hand, your advertising dollars won't get you free publicity, either. You're in an arena where you play by the same rules as everyone else, and media rules are made by professionals: the journalists. Dealing with the media resembles every other game; you need to know the rules to play successfully.

Understanding how reporters operate -- and why -- helps ensure your side of an issue you're concerned about is presented accurately and fairly. You'll also be able to plan your publicity campaign with a fair degree of certainty. You will know the best ways to ensure coverage.

Reporters have a mystique, even an aura of glamour, about them (especially television news anchors). Journalists have been theater, fictionalized and immortalized in plays, books and movies. This "larger than life" myth gets in the way when you're trying to deal with media as an ordinary business owner who wants publicity.

If you're going to work with media, begin by changing your attitude. Journalists are professionals who happen to be skilled in communication; they're people who know the unwritten rules of media. If they're good journalists, they also know what makes people tick, what people are interested in knowing, and how to dig for a story when necessary.

But always remember this: you have a right to approach them with a newsworthy story.

Like every other business, newspapers, magazines, radio and television stations stay in business only as long as they make a profit. To do so, *we* have to read, listen and watch. Without *us*, they fail. But, we do more than serve as an audience for news; we provide it.

A false glamour...a sense of intimidation...a wary suspicion and lack of trust. All are common attitudes that get in the way when you're dealing with media, and when you want their cooperation.

This distrust...and sometimes, outright fear... is more widespread than I had ever realized before I took an informal survey of two different groups in Arizona. The extent of the cynicism I found is meaningful.

For example, out of a total of nearly 240 college juniors and seniors questioned over a period of three years, more than 75 percent categorically said they did *not* trust the accuracy of news stories, whether printed or broadcast. It made no difference whether the media were national or local, although the students tended to put more trust in small community weekly newspapers, "because they know what's going on." More than half the students said they personally knew someone who had been burned by a media story that concerned them.

When I repeated the survey with up-and-coming young leaders in rural Arizona towns, I discovered the disbelief was equally strong. The only substantial difference? *Ninety percent* said they knew someone who had to deal with what they believed were inaccurate stories in the media!

For 30 years, I've worked with reporters from newspapers and magazines, with on-camera reporters from television and on-air radio news people. With rare exception ...and believe me, they *were* rare...journalists worked as hard as they could to make sure their stories were accurate. Four years of college journalism training emphasize accurate, objective, ethical reporting.

Young journalists are idealistic. They believe if people know the "truth," people will make the "right" decisions. And, of course, they, as journalists, will expose the "truth." That attitude is as unrealistic as those held by the media-consuming public.

So, what's the problem? Misunderstanding and mis-communication. On both sides.

Journalists worked as hard as they could to make sure their stories were accurate.

Take a good look at today's news. Watch television with a critical eye...and listen to radio with your full attention. What you see and hear is a mixture...good news and bad, heart-warming and soul-searing, vital and trivial. How you define news depends on your individual viewpoint. That's true for you *and* for journalists.

Your opinion about journalistic accuracy and objectivity changes, particularly when the story concerns you directly.

■ You believe you were quoted in a misleading way. Yes, you said it, but you thought the microphone was off or the interview was over. (The reporter believes you were being honest. Besides, it was the only unequivocal sentence you said all afternoon.)

■ Your quote was used out of context...you meant what you said, but not quite *that* way...it's a complicated situation, and the reporter didn't explain necessary details and ramifications. (The reporter was on a tight deadline, and the editor decided to print only 600 words, instead of the 800 the reporter wrote.)

■ Someone you know was killed in an accidental shooting, and the reporters were right there, intruding in people's grief. This is a common complaint, particularly about television.

(Reporters say that news is news, and the public has a right to know. You might argue their definition of news, but they *are* correct when they say the public is interested, albeit morbidly.) Remember, if this ever happens to you: This is the one situation in which you have every right to say, "No comment" as you slam the door shut.

■ The name of your company was mentioned favorably, but a competitor received top billing...four paragraphs to your two. (The reporter was able to get short, to-the-point quotes from your competitor. Or, your competitor sent over a good photograph without being asked. Or, it could just have been a coincidence.) By the way, no one but you and your competitor will even notice the placement if it happens only once. People simply don't read as carefully as you do when your name is mentioned.

■ You wanted a story on the front page of a particular section of the newspaper, and you were unfairly relegated to an inside page where fewer people will notice you. Good story, but the reporter *promised* you the front page.

(If the reporter actually promised you the cover page, you have a justifiable complaint. Reporters don't decide where their stories will be placed, especially on daily papers. Editors on the city desk are responsible for the make-up of the news pages. Inserts that only appear once a week are designed on a different basis, and a "cover story" may be assigned on a specific topic well ahead of time.)

▪ You sent them a news release, but they didn't print it. (Why not? There could be many, many reasons. Read the rest of the book!)

▪ You were just trying to be helpful when you asked to read over the article before it was printed. The reporter was amused. (Or insulted? Professional editors check reporters' copy. Remember, deadlines are tight; newspapers won't delay the printing process so you can quibble about your story. At least, that's the way *they* look at your request.)

The way the media business works causes misunderstandings. Reporters are trained to be journalists; they learn to write or to appear in front of the camera. They learn how to track down stories, get the information and write the story in a way it can be understood, supposedly by a reader with an eighth-grade education. They are not trained in your business, whatever it may be.

You always have the responsibility to explain your business clearly without jargon when you talk to reporters.

You always have the responsibility to explain your business clearly, without jargon, when you talk to reporters. What they don't understand, they can't explain to a public who understands even less clearly. Good reporters will keep asking until they are sure they know exactly what you're talking about, but even they get hurried and take shortcuts.

At large, metropolitan daily newspapers, reporters rotate from one "desk" to another; they may report on business news for six months, get switched to the police "beat" for awhile, and end up covering the environmental news or the local health and science scene. This constant rotation can go on for years, or the reporter may be fortunate enough to find a niche, becoming the paper's expert on a specific subject.

In addition, reporters face daily deadlines; they must write in a constant hurry. Despite popular beliefs, most reporters rarely have the luxury for true investigative reporting. They seldom can spend months learning about one topic in great depth except at the largest national daily papers, such as the New York Times or the Washington Post or the Los Angeles Times.

At small, weekly newspapers, reporters may cover the general news called-in by their readers...plus the schools...plus the local business community...and even the city hall and police. These reporters are true generalists and they have a finger on the pulse of their community. Whatever happens, they know about it. They can't necessarily print it, but they *know*. This fact in no way relieves you of the responsibility to explain clearly.

Small radio stations are somewhat different. The staff often are responsible for getting advertising accounts, as well as the news. Today, many small stations play music they buy from a remote service; the only truly local programming is news, ads, and occasional talk shows.

What's true for print journalists is even more so for television reporters. They flit from interview to interview every day, hoping to bring out an interesting sound bite (a 15-second, verbal pithy quote) in a picturesque setting so they can get on the air that day. All too often, the system, especially in a small-to-medium-size market, leans toward hype (they exaggerate the story...make it seem world-shattering) and insensitivity ("Let's get the grieving family on-camera").

The journalistic theory of "balanced reporting" causes more misunderstandings than any other practice. In print media, "balance" means that all sides of a controversy are given a chance to state their position. You, the reader, are supposed to have enough information to make up your own mind. Theoretically, balanced reporting *is* objective reporting.

Theoretically, balanced reporting is objective reporting.

You may not see it that way because you are emotionally and intellectually committed to a particular viewpoint. If you are strongly committed, you may regard it as evidence of journalistic bias if the "other" sides are even mentioned. If you think I'm exaggerating, listen to the outraged phone calls to media for a few days. It happens all the time, even when most people wouldn't find the stories at all controversial.

Or, you may believe that the other side is getting a better press. You may be right. Your "opponents" may be presenting their side more clearly. "They" may be making arguments not based on facts; it has happened. Reporters are supposed to be totally objective, but they're human. Newspapers take editorial positions favoring one side of an issue, and almost invariably, reporters take the same side...or move to another newspaper.

"Bias" influences news coverage, but not nearly as often as you may believe.

Start your relationship with the media on a positive note. Believe you're on the same side: *you* have information that the public needs and wants to know; *media* are in the business of getting that information to the public.

The Real World

The occasion was dedicating a new university building. Hardly a media event, especially since the building had already been dedicated twice when VIPs had been on campus. Each time, we'd notified the media...as ordered by the university higher-ups. And, the reporters had responded with a bored ho-hum.

The third dedication was the charm as far as news coverage was concerned. Since the publicity had been lackluster, the higher-up decided to call the publisher himself, bypassing his PR staff. He mentioned the name of the building, and that provided the news spark.

The university had named the building after a beneficent alumni, now deceased, who was rumored involved (though never indicted) in the widely publicized murder of an investigative reporter a decade ago. The third dedication hit the front page, and the publicity was definitely not favorable.

The moral?   Listen to the professionals. Sometimes being greedy for news coverage does not pay off.

How Media Organize

(Why You Should Care)

Like any business, media are organized so they can produce their product efficiently...and profitably. Don't ever forget, all media outlets are in their business for one reason...to make money. They are profitable when they provide a service...information...that enough people are willing to pay for. Undeniably, a free press is a cornerstone of our society. But, that fact does not exempt media from the "laws" of a capitalistic society.

You need to know *how* their organization works because the media are your customers for news about your company. And obviously, the more you know about any customer, the better you are able to serve...and sell to...them.

OWNERSHIP

Once upon a time, newspapers, television and radio stations were locally owned. Each magazine had a separate owner. Today, that's seldom true. Even small-town weekly newspapers with a circulation of 5,000 or less are usually owned by a chain, just like ABCO, Sears or Wal-Mart.

The reasons for the shift in ownership are complicated, but for the most part, it comes down to money. For example, as the communications industry became more high-tech...with computer systems, high-volume, high-speed printing equipment and television camera systems...costs became as astronomical as satellite access. Larger companies could share those expenses.

What difference does it make *who* owns the media? Once upon a time, if you had a complaint, you could invite the editor-publisher for a cup of coffee, argue it out and settle the problem then and there. Your local media managers may still be empowered to settle your complaint...usually that will be true...but not always. It's a bit like doing business with the federal government rather than the county. When the editors say, "I *can't* do that;" they mean it. They can't.

Corporate ownership can have another effect on local media. If the chain's profits decrease...for whatever reason...the local staff will feel the pinch. Reporters won't be replaced when they leave; the number of pages or the use of color photographs may be limited.

Budget cutbacks may force fewer local radio news broadcasts or talk shows because these require local staffing. Music can be done long-distance. The *number* and *length* of newscasts on television stations will probably stay the same, but fewer reporters will cover the news. Also remote (telecast away from the station) broadcasts will be limited; they're more expensive to produce.

Whether you're trying to get broadcast or print publicity, these reductions will make it more difficult for you.

NEWSPAPER ORGANIZATION

The larger the newspaper, the larger the staff and the more layers of editors in the organization. Let's compare national and state (Arizona) papers.

▪ The New York Times has a Sunday circulation of more than 1.6 million. In addition to 10 corporate officers, 12 general managers, separate circulation, advertising and production staffs, the Times has ten news and editorial executives and 28 department editors and managers.

▪ The Arizona Republic, Arizona's largest daily (Sunday circulation greater than 500,000), is based in Phoenix and owned by Central Newspapers Inc. of Indianapolis (former vice president Dan Quayle is a director). The Republic has an executive vice president and general manager, four managing editors, a news editor and seven city and assistant city editors, with 30 different departments. Some department editors have responsibility for more than one desk. The Republic had satellite bureaus in other parts of Arizona, but they have recently been reduced. They also publish different editions for Scottsdale, Mesa, Glendale and north Phoenix communities.

▪ The Yuma Daily Sun is locally owned with a circulation of 24,000. In addition to six departmental or desk editors, the Sun has an editor, plus managing, associate and city editors.

▪ The Mohave Daily Miner, Kingman, AZ, is owned by Western Newspapers, Inc., and has a circulation of nearly 7,000. An editor, news and city editors are in charge of 21 departmental desk editors, most of whom are responsible for four or more departments.

▪ New Times, Phoenix owned and published, advertises itself as the largest free weekly, with a circulation around 140,000. The Times has four department editors (one of them responsible for "News Tips") and six managing or city desk editors.

▪ The Copper Era, a weekly newspaper in Clifton, AZ, is the only newspaper covering Greenlee County. Owned by Wick Communications, the Era has a circulation of slightly more than 3,000 and an editorial staff of one.

Confused? What do all these editors do? More important, which editors should *you* contact when you have a story idea?

Let's start with reporters, the people you're most likely to interact with. Reporters are sometimes called "the foot soldiers" of the journalistic world. They research the news articles, go out and interview, and write the stories that appear, after they've been edited, of course.

At a newspaper, the hub of all the activity is the newsroom. And yes, desks are still crammed messily together, phones ringing, and reporters running. Only computers have replaced the manual typewriter...and reporters, male or female, seldom wear hats.

Reporters answer to a city editor or, on larger papers, to any one of a number of assistant city editors. The news editor takes care of wire service copy and, if the paper is a large metropolitan daily, reports from various correspondents. Feature editors keep track of upcoming feature stories, which are soft news about local people. Newsroom editors work under the managing editor (ME) who, in turn, answers to the editor-in-chief. The publisher is at the head of the chain, but he (with rare exception, the publisher *is* a male) supposedly doesn't interfere with the daily management.

General managers, managing editors, editorial editors, copy editors, news editors are management positions at larger newspapers. In most cases, you will not deal with them directly. If you're uncertain about which department (desk) your news involves, contact the city editor and ask.

Each department editor serves a different constituency and will want to know what your story means in terms of those readers. It can get a bit complicated. Business news usually goes to the business desk, but some daily papers also have an economics desk. If your business is real estate...or science...or interior design, perhaps you should direct your news to those departments.

The departmental editor makes assignments to reporters on that desk or "beat." However, larger newspapers have columnists who write regular, signed columns on specific subject areas...local politics, economics, the environment, sports, business. Often, columnists work more independently than reporters, but either may receive assignments from their department.

If you aren't sure of all the angles involved in your story, you can play it safe by talking with the city editor. Or, you can go directly to several departmental editors. Make sure they know that you've talked to several editors. On large papers, editors may not know who's working on what if it's not on their beat. You might be very happy to have your story appear twice in the same paper on the same day, but the editors will be extremely unhappy, and that could affect your chances of future cooperation.

Time is always a vital consideration for daily newspapers.

Should you contact an individual reporter...cut out the people in the middle? Probably not, although your specific circumstances can make a difference. If you've worked with one individual several times, go ahead and check out your idea. However, reporters will usually be involved on assigned stories (and deadlines). They'll have to take your idea to their editor and you may not have saved any time in getting coverage.

Time is always a vital consideration for daily newspapers. Of course, if you send a written news release or news lead, all you have to worry about is getting it to the paper in a timely fashion (and we'll talk more that in Chapter 3). If you use the telephone or drop by the paper in person to sell your story, find out when your paper goes to press. The very *worst* time to call (or appear) is immediately before that.

In general, morning daily papers have news deadlines in the early to middle of the evening before the date of the paper. Just to complicate matters even more, metropolitan dailies often print more than one edition, and their deadlines will vary. The best time to call is the middle of the afternoon.

Afternoon daily papers publish early in the morning, so the best time for a call or personal visit is in the early afternoon.

Except for late-breaking news, much of the Sunday paper is written, by the same busy reporters, during the week in the supposed lull between daily editions. Some sections, such as the travel, home and lifestyle, are printed ahead of time, but the news sections go to press Saturday afternoon, and the same guidelines for seeing editors apply as for any other day of the week.

Notice, the times I've given are general. Your best bet is checking with the city editor of the specific paper.

On smaller papers...non-metropolitan dailies and small-town weeklies...your concern is not *who* to contact. Simply call or send your release to the news editor. *When* is just as important as it is for the larger daily papers. Traditionally, weekly papers are published for distribution on Wednesday because that's the day supermarkets want to advertise. Get your news to the editor a week ahead of time; they're least frantic on Thursday or Friday because this week's paper is finished. Again, check. Your paper may differ.

MAGAZINE ORGANIZATION

You have an ever-growing selection of magazines to choose from, but in general, you can divide magazines into two categories when you're thinking about publicity: trade magazines and consumer-oriented magazines. We'll ignore other categories, such as news weeklies. If your publicity is <u>that</u> newsworthy, they'll probably contact you. And, you should be working with PR professionals to make sure your news gets adequate coverage.

Every trade, every profession has its own trade magazines. They don't have the circulation of such consumer-oriented magazines as Better Homes & Gardens or Redbook, but they are much easier for you to access, and they may be a valuable way to gain credibility with your customers.

No matter what the category or what the circulation, magazines are organized in similar ways. An editorial staff is headed by an editor-in-chief, with section editors responsible for various parts of the magazine. In small trade magazines, one or two editors may constitute the entire staff.

Editors decide on the articles to be used; the writers may be hired full-time by the magazine or free-lance writers may be assigned on an article-by-article, issue-by-issue basis. The same is true for photographers. In-house editors and graphic designers put the final magazine together.

The greatest organizational difference between trade and consumer magazines is the size of the staff; trade magazines usually operate on a shoestring.

In either case, before you write the article you have in mind, read several issues to make certain your idea really fits. Then (and only then) send a *query letter* to the magazine editor, describing (and selling) your idea. The editor will decide whether your idea is appropriate.

A word about magazine deadlines: editors work *months* ahead, not days or weeks. If you have a holiday-related publicity idea, query the editors nine months ahead. Editors have the focus of their magazines planned at least three, and usually six months in advance. Remember, we're not talking about weekly news magazines.

BROADCAST MEDIA ORGANIZATION

Radio:

Radio stations are either AM or FM, a designation referring to their broadcast frequency and power. Most FM stations offer a music format. Radio stations are generally organized along two formats. Consider the formats of Christian and non-English stations individually.

■ Talk or news radio stations feature exactly that: talk and call-in shows and frequent news updates. They offer more opportunities for your publicity efforts.

■ Stations that feature music cater to people with different tastes: Top 40, Golden Oldies, Heavy Metal, Adult Contemporary, Easy Listening, Country Western, etc. These stations also have brief news broadcasts, usually on an hourly basis. Any publicity for them has to interest their specific market segment. Also, the announcement will be brief, probably no more than 15 seconds.

The majority of radio stations have very small news operations. The music they provide is usually canned; the local disk jockey does continuity between selections, reads the local ads, announces the time and weather, and sometimes also is the news announcer. The news comes from a teletype machine from a wire service.

Only the very largest metropolitan radio stations have enough news reporters to send them outside the station on stories. Even stations with more than one news reporter rely on the telephone to get local news. News directors are in charge; call them. The best time is immediately following a news broadcast. Be prepared to have your voice recorded over the phone and replayed during the news broadcast.

Many radio stations also have a Public Affairs Director in charge of such things as community calendars; contact this person to get listed. Each talk show has its own host and producer (sometimes the same person); contact them to get scheduled on their show.

Television:

Today, viewers have a choice of television stations that has multiplied like the proverbial rabbit...and shows no sign of slowing down. The ability to choose among 500 stations is predicted for the near future. Unfortunately (or perhaps fortunately) you won't be able to place your news or publicity with equal ease...or results...on all 500.

The number of people buying cable television service continues to increase.

Except for CNN channels, cable television channels (such as AMC, ARTS, BET, DISC, MTV, TLC, etc.) rarely have news or local publicity shows. However, buying local advertising time is less expensive than buying time even on local network affiliates. Cable channels are proliferating, offering more choices to audiences with narrow ranges of interest, whether it's rock and roll or science fiction or 24-hour animated comics. The number of people buying cable television service continues to increase.

Local network affiliates are associated with ABC, CBS and NBC; they contract with the network for national programming. Affiliates also produce local news shows and some talk shows. Until recently, the networks were the only game in town, and the affiliates took whatever the networks offered, but that's less and less true.

Local network affiliates are associated with ABC, CBS and NBC; they contract with the network for national programming. Affiliates also produce local news shows and some talk shows. Until recently, the networks were the only game in town, and the affiliates took whatever the networks offered, but that's less and less true.

I use the word "local," but that may be deceptive. Most network affiliates broadcast from metropolitan areas, and are rebroadcast through microwave into rural areas. If you're in a smaller town, your access to news and talk shows is more difficult.

Independent networks, such as Fox, offer another choice for viewers, but are not a publicity outlet for you except through paid advertising.

Public Broadcast channels, such as PBS, are an opportunity if you're lucky enough to have such a station nearby. They are usually associated with a university, and they have a devoted following, albeit a small one. These stations always have some time set aside for local programming.

Don't confuse PBS with local educational channels used for teaching purposes by community colleges and universities. They are rarely open to your news or publicity efforts. Teaching a course may be an option if you have the time and credentials, but that possibility goes beyond publicity considerations.

Public Access Channels are set aside by local authorities who require that cable companies make them available. And so they are, but their viewing audience is extremely limited.

Whether you're dealing with a **PBS** or a network affiliate, decide whether you're trying to place an item on the news show or if you want to be on a talk show. It makes a big difference as far as the person you should contact.

Who determines what is news (and what gets covered that day) depends on the size of the news-gathering operation. Larger stations use their *news director* as an administrator not directly connected with the day-to-day operation. At smaller stations, the news director may be the producer, the assignment director and the news anchor.

Usually, the person who calls the shots...the one for you to contact...is the *assignment director*. He or she decides which stories the film crews and reporters will cover, on a day-to-day, even hour-to-hour basis. Generally, on-air reporters have no say about which stories are covered, but they have great control over how your story is treated. The *news producer* works in the control room at the studio; he or she may write what the anchor will say, assembles the pictures that flash up behind the anchor at the beginning of the story and determines the order of the stories in the newscast.

As at newspapers, television news deadlines are a daily occurrence. To get on the evening news, the film crews and reporters must have shot the story during the morning or early afternoon, unless the story is done live during the broadcast. "Live" stories are reserved for breaking news, such as a fire.

If you have a timely news story, contact the assignment director the day before...at the latest. The best time is after the daily assignments are made...usually about 11 a.m. **Don't** call in the afternoon when the news crews are hectically putting together the evening news broadcast.

If your story is less time-oriented -- if it could be covered any time this month, for example -- be sure to tell the director. If you are trying to get coverage of a specific event, give the director more than one day's notice.

Who should you contact if you're trying to be a guest on a talk show? Every such show has a producer, but *talk show producers* are in the *program department*, not the news department. They select the guests who will appear on the show, schedule advance interviews and brief the hosts about questions, demonstrations, etc. Therefore, contact the producer, not the on-air host.

The Real World

Neither logic — nor any journalistically accepted sense of what's newsworthy -- rules on television news. Just watch any local news broadcast to see what I mean. Some of the damnedest stories are covered, especially at the end of the half-hour and particularly when the rest of the news of the day has been particularly grim. The news producers want you to leave with a warm, fuzzy feeling, I guess.

That must be why I was able to place a rope-jumping contest on the late night news. Or why the 12-foot-long hero sandwich made by a local restaurant rated a spot. And the 90-year-old bungee jumper. And as sure as the weather warms in the spring, TV news will feature the birth of some cute furry mammal at the local zoo.

A few years ago, the Parker, AZ, 4-H clubs sponsored a springtime frog-jumping contest a la Mark Twain, with one added feature. If you didn't own your own frog, they'd rent you one.

Tongue firmly in cheek, I sent out a release about the "Rent-a-frog 4-H Jumping Contest." A Phoenix TV station sent a crew more than 200 miles to Parker to broadcast the event. Even more amazing, I had a call from a network national headquarters in New York. They were considering sending their national weatherman to Parker!

Moral: Think creatively about publicity. You could make the evening news.

Free Publicity

Publicity Rules

1. Focus on the right audience-the people who need to know about your business. Know them well enough that you also know the best media to use to reach them and the kinds of information that will most powerfully motivate them.

2. Be newsworthy Offer the media information about events or projects that truly deserve publicity. Puffery without substance won't appeal to the media or the people you're trying to reach. It won't help your credibility, either.

3. Select one person to be in charge of your publicity campaign and limit the number of people who must approve. Publicity by committee is always ineffective. Be careful about setting responsibility for publicity around an event you're planning.

4. Choose the most appropriate media to reach your particular target. Stay local unless you really need wider coverage. Mass media aren't always your best choice. If you're trying to reach a small, very specific audience, use their newsletters, bulletins-whatever reaches them.

5. Make a Calendar Keep track of details and start early if you're publicizing an event. If your event is annual, consider using a professional photographer or videographer this year to help you with publicity next year.

6. Be Brief Limit your news releases announcing events and awards to one, double-spaced page. Features and magazine articles may be longer. Ask magazine editors for the length article they want.

7. Establish good media contacts. Learn their deadlines and always respect them. Learn by name who to contact at specific broadcast stations and newspapers. Be businesslike, but friendly. Limit your calls to ideas you know are newsworthy.

8. Localize your publicity to make it newsworthy to local media. Don't worry about regional or national media unless your project truly deserves such coverage-and you need it to reach your target audience.

9. Follow Up If your project deserves advance publicity, it probably deserves follow-up media coverage. Send a news release to local media. Send it immediately, so the event is still newsworthy.

10. Thank the media for their cooperation. When they do a good job of covering your story, write to the reporters' editors. This happens so seldom that reporters never forget.

Publicity Ideas

News

1. Summarize your annual report, especially any business changes or favorable trends. Be sure to quote your top executive. Send to business sections and magazines; skip broadcast (radio and television).

2. Release a comment or make a speech taking a position on a community, legislative or industry issue. The more the issue is already in the news, and the more it impacts your local community-the greater the news value. Send a speech copy to the média and invite them to attend the occasion, but always send a news release, also.

3. When you reorganize, merge companies, change management, elect new Board of Director members, hire new executives or get major new investors, tell the local business press about it, as well as the trade press in your industry. In the news release, focus on the difference your changes will make to the community and industry.

4. Opening a new branch or office is news, especially if you're creating new job openings for local people. Let the media know as far ahead of time as possible to allow people to apply. Take photographs of your new office during the construction and hold a ribbon cutting ceremony.

5. Changing your plant can be hotter news (and more apt to get coverage) if: 1) it has a positive environmental impact; 2) you've restored a historic site; 3) you're installing innovative production machinery or high-tech equipment that's a first in town. Television news crews will like the visual possibilities.

6. Changing a customer policy may be news if: 1) your change is a first for your industry; 2) it has a measurable impact on all your customers; 3) it particularly affects children. Focus your news release on the impact and the reasons for the change.

7. Announce the results of research you've conducted on your industry trends, your services, products or customers. The more surprising the research results, the better. Announce the changes you'll make as a result. Don't forget your trade press.

8. When someone in your business testifies before Congress or appears at a national meeting, announce the appearance and summarize the speech. Offer to write a one-time, newspaper column. Also offer to appear on radio and TV talk shows.

9. Proudly announce your community relations programs and the affect they're having on local problems. Be sure to feature involved employees in your internal communications as well in the outside publicity. If possible, invite the media to interview someone you've helped.

10. Create a source book of experts in your organization; send to local media. Don't overlook expertise that has little to do with your organization per se. If employees have unusual hobbies or play unusual sports, a news story would feature them but your company name would be mentioned.

11. After someone goes to a national business conference, write a news release commenting on issues and trends raised that affect your community and your industry. Quote the conference speakers and include a quote from your delegate or your CEO.

Send the release to local business papers and to trade magazines that are not otherwise covering the conference.

12. Co-sponsor a workshop with local media on a topic of mutual interest. The workshop itself will probably be covered, but you also will get to know media representatives -- and vice versa.

13. Write a regular column on industry issues (or have a writer prepare the column, using your information). Send the column to your trade press. Rewrite for the general public whenever interest in your topic justifies, and send to local newspapers.

14. Distribute your employee and customer newsletters to the local newspaper editor covering your business. Reporters will occasionally pick up ideas for stories they'll write.

15. Send local print media one- or two-line fillers, using facts, statistics or trivia about your business. Even if your company name isn't mentioned, you'll stand out as an expert from the crowd seeking publicity.

16. What is little-known, unusual and fascinating about your business, your industry or perhaps, some of your employees? Always get their permission before talking to media about them; make sure they realize reporters may want to interview them.

17. List your name as a community resource in local organization's telephone directories. Media often use these directories as a story source.

18. If, over the years, your business or agency has changed in newsworthy ways, let the media know when you celebrate an anniversary. Include nostalgic photographs.

19. Let the media know when you overcome a challenging problem, especially if the crisis is caused by outside forces beyond your control, such as the weather or government regulators. Did you get orders to customers on time despite a fire, flood, or power shut-down?

20. Get national VIPs to visit your business; make sure they're willing to be interviewed by local media. Have them make a speech, greet customers, give a demonstration. What the VIP *does* while visiting your business should be as newsworthy as the VIP if you want to get the best publicity.

Events

21. Create an unusual store-front demonstration or exhibit to arouse customer attention. Then, call the media, especially the television news desk. Be careful about using animals, or you may get the kind of publicity you don't want.

22. Tie the events you promote into holidays in offbeat ways that relate to your business and your clients. (Offer free professional massages or marriage counseling to reduce Christmas stress. Offer a gardening lesson for green thumb people on St. Patrick's Day. etc.)

23. Sponsor a book-signing session in your store, featuring an author who writes about your industry. Ask the author to answer customer questions; publicize that fact.

24. Tie into national publicity materials offered by industry PR. Every day and week has its own theme, ranging from serious health issues (Diabetes Awareness Week) to products (Dairy Day). Arrange a local angle that promotes your business to interest media.

25. Take part in industry trade shows; be willing to talk to reporters who cover the shows. Think ahead, so you can talk knowledgeably about industry trends and issues. Give TV interviews by your booth.

26. Offer to give demonstrations, conduct a workshop or speak when you take part in events sponsored by someone else. Contact whoever is in charge of event publicity to make sure your name and business are mentioned. If necessary, write the news release yourself.

27. Celebrate your anniversaries and milestones; being in business, a product or service you offer, long-term employees, your oldest location, etc. Anniversaries that are multiples of five years are most recognized by the media. Notable milestones include your first million-dollar year, reaching fund-raising goals, 100,000th product off your production line, etc. Celebrate in unusual, very visual ways.

Awards

28. Send local print media a black and white head and shoulders photo, along with a brief (one page maximum) news release whenever you or an employee win a regional or national award. Describe the award, who gave it and the reason you won it. The paper's coverage will be very short, but people will notice.

29. Honor one of your employees each month. Give the same information (and send a photo) as if it were a national award. The award may be given for service within your company or to the community. Send to local print media, the industry trade papers and publicize in employee newsletters.

30. Create a community service award relating to your industry. Present the award with due pomp and ceremony.

Send media coverage of the award and any noteworthy speeches made. Invite media to attend, but provide news releases whether or not they come. Make sure all your employees, stockholders and customers know about your award and the reasons they were won.

Make Publicity Work For You

31. Include local free lance writers on your newsletter list. They're constantly looking for ideas, and they know how to place stories in a wide variety of media.

32. Make sure your employees, investors and selected clients get copies of any media coverage about you, your business and vital issues in your industry. If employees are mentioned by name, send a copy to their families, along with a note of congratulation.

33. Check for favorable media articles that refer to your clients and prospects. Use a clipping service if you don't have time to search. Send clients a copy, with a brief, handwritten congratulatory note.

34. Keep up with new communication technology. Would a radio media tour, done by telephone to radio talk shows statewide fit your publicity needs? Should you work with cable television? Do you have the budget for video news releases, perhaps sent by satellite?

35. Get professional advice. Publicity is not a one-time, impromptu, last-minute try for media coverage. Effective publicity is well-planned, year-round effort.

Planning Guide

Goals Check off this list; add others. The list includes both long- and short-range objectives.

_____ Get more people to an event
_____ Increase customers in present market area
_____ Expand your market into a new area
_____ Introduce a new product or service
_____ Change personal or business image

Target audience Describe your top priority audience. Include income level, gender, age, occupation, location, and any other distinguishing characteristics that help determine the media you choose and the audience-motivators.

Budget Calculate the amount of time and money you can afford to spend on publicity. Include the fee you will pay a professional to develop a publicity plan with you, to write and distribute news releases, plan publicity events and deal with media. Although media publicity is low-cost, it does have a price.

Responsibility Who will be in charge of planning publicity? Who is assigned to contact media? Who will design and create publicity pieces? Who will distribute? Who is in charge of mailing lists? Who will approve publicity materials? Are these duties to be added to their existing workload; if so, who will pick up the overload?

Results What equals success in your campaign?

Media Planning

Newsworthiness What makes your story worthy of coverage by the media? Consider who, what, when, where, why, how. Add visual impact if you want television coverage. Also consider what the particular media consider news.

Media What media are available to you to reach your target audience? Possible options include: daily and weekly papers; trade magazines; association newsletters; radio and/or television newscasts or talk shows.

Contacts Who do you need to contact at the specific media you've chosen? Get names and telephone numbers of the appropriate editors. Be sure you're contacting the right person, as well as the best media. Find out if you need to write a query letter, a proposal or merely call.

Formats Choose the best format for your publicity. Your options include: news releases; news leads; media kits; feature articles; regular columns; press conferences; letters to the editors; radio scripts; and personal appearances.

Timetable When does your publicity need to appear if it is going to help you reach your goals? How long will it take you to plan, prepare and produce the necessary materials? Start at the ending date and work backwards. The more complicated your plan, the more time you need.

People Planning

Interviews Who should-and is prepared to-give interviews to the media about your particular publicity? If a reporter calls, who should answer? The person you assign to give interviews depends on who is most knowledgeable-who has the best media presence (this is especially important for radio and television)-and who has the time. Remember, reporters may need to interview more than one person.

Visuals Decide ahead of time what photographic or graphic possibilities exist. Newspapers will want to assign their own photographer, but magazines may want you to provide. Then, you need to know what format they want. Should you hire a professional photographer?

Action Television stations want action shots, especially if you hope to get news coverage. Can you stage the action? What facilities will you need? More important, what facilities do the station videographers want? And, who is involved in the "action?"

Production Who will design, produce and print the necessary media materials? Who will distribute them? Who will coordinate your media publicity production? Who will approve the materials? Make these decisions ahead of time to avoid mass confusion.

Publicity Coverage

The publicity you're trying to generate has to fit into a news category before the media will consider using it. To the media, news happens in two categories: hard and soft. Think of it this way: *Hard news* is happening now; it's urgent. Fires, floods, tornadoes, mine disasters, random shootings where several people are killed, tax increases (or decreases), court and jury decisions...all these are hard news. You notice that hard news is often negative news.

Soft news is sometimes called *features*; it generally has no tight time deadline. It will still be a good story next week. Soft news often involves human interest details. The same story may involve both, and the more dramatic the news, the more likely it does.

The mine disaster in Superior, Arizona, in August 1993 is an example. Four miners were killed between 9 and 11 p.m. when tons of ore and rock fell on them as they worked 4,000 feet underground. The "hard" news of the disaster...who was killed, where, how it happened, rescue attempts, along with a color photograph of grieving relatives and a drawing of the mine shaft...were the main front page story in the next morning's daily paper in the Tucson Arizona Daily Star.

Sharing the front page was a feature story about the youngest miner killed, a 19-year-old. His family, his young daughter, his neighbors were interviewed, and the story featured a wedding photograph. On page four of the front section, another feature story profiled the oldest miner killed; again a photograph, a candid shot taken with his wife in their home, was used. Another story, on page five, included a listing of mine accidents since 1982 in Arizona and featured two black and white photos of the shaft at the mine entrance and lowering the flags after the disaster.

By the time the afternoon daily, Tucson Citizen, came out, the mine disaster still rated front page coverage, but it no longer was the first story. The article focused on interviews with the surviving relatives, with a hard news story on the accident's cause relegated to the fifth page.

Television coverage began with the 10 p.m. evening news, before any remote crews could reach the mine. The anchor read a brief announcement. The coverage continued the following day with video shot at the scene, but the story came later in the newscast.

As long as the media believed readers and viewers were interested in the disaster, the coverage continued. Within a week, the mine disaster was reduced to funeral coverage, but the story was again news when authorities placed the blame at least partially on the mining company. For one day, the disaster was front page news.

The Midwestern 1993 summer floods are an example of long-continued hard and soft news coverage.

When a disaster takes over the front page, all other news is shoved aside to make room. Your story won't make it into the front section of the paper that day unless it relates to the headline news. Usually, the other sections...sports, lifestyle, business, international news...are unaffected.

The "softer" your publicity story, the harder you will have to work to sell it to the news editors. Their first duty as journalists is to cover the hard news, and they usually have more to choose from than they have room in the paper.

Since radio news takes up only a few minutes each hour, the news editor is even less likely to be interested in soft, feature-type news. Go ahead, try to place your idea on radio, but make sure your idea is truly unique, or vitally important for the people in the station's audience. On the other hand, radio news staffs have shrunk greatly in the past few years. If you are willing to be interviewed over the phone, or if you send a professional-quality audio tape in an acceptable format, your chances of getting on air are quite high.

In theory, television journalists have the same dedication to hard news. The harder the news, the closer to the beginning of the newscast it goes. True, but in reality they look for stories with stronger visual aspects and few details. Television is the medium of impressions; stories are covered in a very few minutes; facts get glossed over in favor of the more visually impressive. The birth of a baby elephant at the zoo will get TV news air time because people will stay tuned to coo over the new baby, not because it's important hard news.

To sell your publicity, try to tie into hard news stories that are breaking, either locally, regionally or nationally. For example, if you had a product that signals miners when rocks are unstable and ready to fall, August 1993 was the time to get publicity in Arizona. If your product helps clean the muck out of flooded houses, you'd have received media interest even in non-flooded parts of the country.

Hard news is happening now...
it's urgent.
Soft news often involves
human interest details.

Also, be aware of the varying needs of the different media. An editor of a small town newspaper is interested in what's happening in that town because the subscribers are interested. If the teenage daughter of one of the residents goes to summer camp...that's news. When someone has an award-winning flower display at the county fair...that's news. When the founder's son takes over the local drugstore...that's news. For a metropolitan paper, all these items occur too frequently and routinely for coverage.

All right, you're aware of some of the complications in defining "news" and deciding who will be interested in your publicity story. But, what *is* news? Basically, "news" equals information that people *want* to know more about or *need* to know...as defined by the news organization. If you believe you have a story that should be told, ask yourself:

- Is it local?
- Is it unusual? Unique? What's different about your story?
- How timely is it? If your story isn't reported this week, will people still be interested?
- How are people touched, involved, entertained or concerned?
- Which people? How many? Where are they?
- Are children involved? Are animals involved? Is the environment involved?
- Does your story help people save money? Or, does it protect them from losing money? How much?
- Does your information help people solve a problem...or inform them about a problem they haven't heard of before?
- Does your story tie into another story getting media attention? Is it part of a trend? Are famous (or infamous) people involved?
- Why do people need to know? This is the most basic question of all, and the one that's the easiest to forget.

Obviously, the more news factors your story involves, the more likely you'll get media publicity. Still, the nature of the news business can interfere. I've written enough about deadline pressure that you realize journalists are *always* in a hurry. No matter how good your story is, you may still get these excuses:

- "We'd like to cover your story, but every reporter is busy today."
- "That's a good story, but we're full up today. The whole newscast is already scheduled."

■ "Usually we'd cover your story, but we have our hands full with the election, and some other breaking news."

Excuses? Sure, but they're usually true, anyway. What should you do about it? Don't give up; don't take the rejection personally. Look at your story again.

■ Can you find another angle that will place it in another newspaper department to reach your desired audience? Can you interest a columnist...or write a column yourself?

■ Can you add another dimension to your story? Professional photographs? An additional person to interview? A more attractive visual aspect?

■ Can you sell your publicity story with greater enthusiasm (even if it's the 50th time you've tried)?

Don't give up; Don't take rejection personally.

■ Will another medium work for you? Trade magazines? A talk show instead of the news? A speech to an interested group? A newsletter? A billboard?

■ Can you afford to wait a week or a month to place the story?

■ Have you brainstormed your publicity idea with someone who's not as close to your business as you are?

PUBLICITY STORY CHECKLIST

Before you plan the details of your publicity campaign, think through and answer the following checklist items.

My goals for this publicity are:
_____ Get larger attendance for an event
_____ Promote a new product or service
_____ Inform people about a change in address, employees or management
_____ Expand my market into a new area
_____ Educate people about my products
_____ Get support for a community project
_____ Become personally better known as an expert
_____ Enhance my company's reputation
_____ Other?

For each goal, list the result that equals success. How will I measure that success? Be specific.

Who are my top priority target audiences? Describe their demographics as fully as possible (age, income, location, business, etc.)

Describe the media they are most likely to pay attention to. Include local newspapers, both dailies and weeklies, local radio and television stations, regular and trade magazines, and community papers or newsletters. If appropriate, include regional or national media.

List all the facts of the publicity story.

Who can the media interview about my story? Give their titles and why media would be interested.

What are the photographic possibilities? (For print media)

What are sound possibilities? (For radio)

List the visual and action possibilities and their location. (For television)

List of questions reporters might want to ask.

The Real World

For once I had a story with some real meat...a story with good media publicity angles. The population of a tiny insect, the whitefly, had exploded into astronomical numbers. Carl Sagan's term "billions and billions" was a reality in Arizona. And everyone was worried. Cotton and vegetable farmers were suffering severe damage, and even urban Phoenicians were complaining about insect problems.

Since we were part of the agricultural science community, we held local farmer meetings around the state to explain our research into whitefly controls. *Local media covered the meetings.*

We wrote news releases and many magazine articles. *All were printed.* We held news conferences when the research results justified, and we made our scientists available for media interviews. *All were well attended and the scientists complained of having too much coverage.*

Moral: When you have a good topic, cover all media bases.

Making Contact

I've described how various media are organized; here's where you start using that information. Now that you know *what* your publicity idea is and *who* it's aimed at and *why*, you're just about ready to get in touch with the media.

Start by making a list of local media contacts. If your publicity idea has national implications, get names of contacts from national media directories. Check the list of media directories and mailing list sources at the end of this chapter. This is not an all-inclusive list, by the way. These are expensive resources; most of them cost between $200 and $500 per year. Unless you're planning a continued use of national media that would make the expense worthwhile, see if your local library has the directories.

Your initial contact should always be with the assignment director or the appropriate news editor. Names change; people move from job to job. It's embarrassing...and certainly unprofessional...to send a hot publicity tip to an editor who left the paper two years ago. You *could* send your information to the job title, but take the time to find the name of the person in the job. Locally, that's easy to do; use your phone book to call the paper, station or channel. Ask the receptionist. Get the proper spelling and their telephone number if they have a separate line. Make a list for your Rolodex ™ and update it every six months.

Now, put your office filing system to use. Keep track of all the story ideas you suggest...the angle you suggest...and the editors you approach. If you make a phone call and say you're going to send a release or a media kit, make a note in your file. And follow up. Then, add the editor's reaction to your file. Also keep a file of articles you read that prompt an idea you can take advantage of...tomorrow, if not today.

Publicizing an Event

Getting media publicity about an event you've scheduled can be one of the easier publicity projects. The rules for getting coverage are easily explained, too. But before you start planning your publicity campaign strategy, ask yourself, "Is this meeting or event going to present worthwhile information people really *need* to know?" Nothing will hurt your credibility more...with your audience and with the media...than a highly publicized event that just doesn't amount to much. All too often, egos get in the way. Look at the goals you've set for your publicity, and make sure you stick with them.

You're certainly entitled to hold private meetings that are restricted to an invited few, unless you're part of the government in a state with an open meeting law. But, media prefer to announce and cover meetings that are open to the public, for a simple reason. Public meetings are of more interest to readers and viewers.

Once again, the media differ in their willingness to announce events. Many daily and weekly newspapers and most community radio stations have several regular places in which they announce meetings open to the public. Trade magazines always have a calendar of upcoming events in their industry.

Except for some public access channels, television stations rarely announce meetings, with one exception. They sometimes will publicize meetings about public issues of wide and controversial interest. Usually those events are called by an official. Since network affiliates usually broadcast to a large area, they can't afford the air time to announce all the events going on.

I strongly believe that any event worth announcing in advance is worthy of follow-up publicity.

Go back to your original publicity plan to see which target audience you are really aiming at. Look at their demographics. The media you choose to contact to publicize your event depends on that target. However, if you just want the greatest possible attendance without regard to *who* they are, try to get your meeting announcement on the radio stations and in the Sunday newspaper (it has the greatest circulation).

Remember, weekly or small community papers will only announce your meeting if it involves *their* readers.

If you're aiming at people with very specific interests or businesses, consider using the calendar in the trade magazines. You might also try to place a feature story about you and the reason for your event in the magazine and in the business section.

Even if they're not interested in promoting attendance, perhaps you can persuade editors to cover the event and write a follow-up story. In fact, I strongly believe that any event worth announcing in advance is worthy of follow-up publicity.

■ Timing: Plan ahead. Get all your promotional materials ready before you start contacting media. If magazines are part of your media mix, contact them first...at least two, and preferably three, months in advance. Best of all, check with the particular magazines for their deadlines.

Inform daily newspaper features editors and weekly editors at least three weeks early and send information for a calendar-type listing about two weeks early. You want to give: 1) the paper time to list your event; 2) people who want to attend time to make up their minds; and 3) editors time to decide on feature coverage.

If you want television stations to send camera teams to your meeting, use a slightly different approach to the assignment editor. Talk to the editor approximately one week in advance. You have the best chance of success if:
■ your topic is controversial and/or very important to the community;
■ your speakers are well-known;
■ your topic is very important to your area;
■ children, animals or the environment are concerned;

- you're dealing with something new and startling;
- something "visual" will take place.

News Conference

Correctly used, a *news conference* can generate publicity in all your targeted media at the same time with just one event. Unfortunately, news conferences seldom are correctly used, and the media have become justifiably cynical about them. By definition, when you call a news (or press) conference, you invite all the press and radio and television reporters in an area to gather for a news announcement that they won't otherwise be able to get.

If you want to hold a successful news conference, *only* schedule one when:

- you have a significant, important, timely news announcement to make that will make a major impact on people in the area;
- you're announcing a mega-event to take place at a definite time in the fairly near future;
- you or someone in your business has become a political candidate;
- you are willing to answer questions from reporters attending the conference.

To get reporters to your conference, you must give editors enough information about your announcement that they will come to the conference, yet not enough that reporters can do the story without being there. That's a tricky mix because the media have been burned by unkept promises. More and more, editors have a policy that equals: "If you don't tell us who's going to be at the conference and what announcement they'll make, we won't come. "

All too frequently, news conferences are held to promote egos, not news. That's why they fail.

Timing

Timing the conference appropriately is vital; remember the conflicting deadlines faced by morning and afternoon newspapers and by television newscasters. Your first consideration is the top priority media market you need to reach.

Early afternoon...before 2 p.m...will allow television stations to edit tapes before the evening news, and the dailies will have the information for the next day's edition.

Since they probably won't send reporters, send a news release to weekly papers and call into radio stations on the same day, but after the conference. Try to take the time to audio-tape a brief interview with one or several of the conference presenters; hand-deliver the tape to the stations. Don't use a tape of the entire conference for this purpose. Radio stations can only use a few seconds, and they won't take the time to edit your tape. You probably won't have time to take care of that editing on the day of your conference.

Have the news release prepared so you also can send it any to media outlets that were invited but didn't come. They won't have as complete a story as those who attended because they missed the question-answer session, but that is their decision.

The day of the week can make a difference in the coverage you receive. Yes, this is getting complicated; that's another reason to think twice about holding a news conference! Unless your announcement is really front-page news, Friday is the worst day to schedule a conference. Much of the copy for Saturday and Sunday papers is already written, and reporters have left for the weekend.

Monday is the best day for a news conference because weekends are often slow news days, and your conference will generate maximum coverage. Tuesday, Wednesday and Thursday are also possibles. If you want reporters to develop feature stories based on the information you give them, holding a Monday conference will give them time to write for the large-circulation Sunday paper.

Media Kit

Assemble a media kit for attending reporters; it gives reporters who come to your conference another edge over those who have to depend on your news release. The kit also allows reporters to develop feature stories.

Your media kit should contain:

■ Background and supportive materials. If a research study relates to your subject, include a copy. Put in any historical information about your company that's relevant.

■ Photographs relating to your subject <u>and</u> mug shots of those taking part.

■ A complete list of the names, titles, work addresses and phone numbers of all people in the conference. Add a brief biographical sketch of these folks (no more than two paragraphs). You may want to list other people not associated with your company who have informed opinions on your subject. If so, make sure these people have agreed to be listed.

■ Any additional information about your project.

■ A brief statement from each of the conference participants...no more than two or three people from your company or project who are very well prepared.

■ A business card from the person responsible for handling all follow-up calls from the media.

Package the entire kit in an attractive...but not flashy...folder that has your company logo on the cover.

Use a similar media kit whenever reporters want information about a story. For that reason, make extra copies of the covers and whatever information about your company, etc., that could be relevant on a continuing basis. Keep your media kit in mind...and updated.

Conference Location

You're not finished preparing for your news conference, yet. Choose its *location* carefully with two criteria in mind; the first is the most important.

- The site should relate to the reason you're holding a conference.
- The location should be centrally located and accessible to the media.

If you're holding the conference inside, make sure the room is large enough to hold the reporters (and the television film crews). Have enough electrical outlets with sufficient power to allow TV and radio reporters to plug in. They have batteries, but reporters appreciate not having to depend on them. Having nearby phones is still important, but cellular phones are so common now you may no longer have to worry about telephones.

Put a convenient table near the entrance for any exhibits or brochures. Arrange for someone to hand every reporter your media kit; don't depend on their picking it up themselves.

Take a careful look at the backdrop behind your presenters. Light glaring in through unshaded windows create gigantic lighting difficulties for TV cameras and photographers.

To avoid the possibility of late mail deliveries, hand-deliver a news lead two days before your scheduled conference to all assignment directors and news editors. Include the local office of wire services such as Associated Press and United Press International. They put out daily event calendars to all their subscribers.

On the morning of your conference, make a brief phone call to all the assignment directors and news editors. Ask if they're sending reporters, but also give them an additional tidbit of information that will increase the likelihood of their attendance.

Obviously, with all these details to keep in mind, you need careful planning and a staff of people, each with a list of responsibilities. Planning takes time. Don't decide today to hold a news conference the day after tomorrow. Allow yourself at least two weeks...preferably one month.

One final note about news conferences: Think very hard before you decide to have a conference. Then, think again. All too frequently, news conferences are held to promote egos, not news. That's why they fail.

The Real World

Anyone who's been in public relations or the media can tell horror stories about the numerous news conferences they've attended. Conferences that died ignominious deaths without ever seeing any coverage.

Examples? The conference called because a university was going to build yet another building...in two years. Or, the time a governor's representative came to the same university just to talk to a vice president.

Or, the conference called because 23 people were visiting from Egypt; their reason for being here was important to them, but not to anyone outside the industry.

Not being noticed by the media lately does not qualify, by itself, as a good reason for scheduling a news conference. Serving an expensive brunch to reporters won't automatically get coverage for the conference. These days, many media reporters are warned *never* to accept freebies so they can't be accused of favoritism later.

Moral: The purpose of a news conference is to announce important news to all your targeted media at the same time. No other purpose will work.

Print Media
Tools of the Trade

The *news lead* is a basic tool you can use to inform newspapers about a story they need to cover. Send a news lead (sometimes called a news tip) when you want reporters to write the story. Use a news lead *instead* of a news release when your publicity story:

- needs feature coverage, rather than shorter hard news coverage;
- concerns several complicated, but important, factors;
- has long-range implications.

If your publicity really should be written by a professional writer, you have two choices. You can interest the professional journalists at target newspapers, or you can hire someone to do your writing, such as a public relations firm or a freelance writer. Start with a news lead to the newspapers.

Smaller non-metropolitan daily newspapers and small-town weekly papers seldom have the space or journalists available for longer, more complicated stories. So, using a news lead is less likely to succeed. As always, you need to check the specific papers you have targeted. You may be able to develop a more personal friendly relationship with an editor at a smaller paper that will lead to a feature story; in this case, your news lead becomes a phone call, rather than written.

The format for a news lead (see Appendix I for an example) is similar to that of a news release, but it's shorter and less restricted to "just the facts, ma'am." The entire purpose of a lead is to motivate the editor to assign your story to a reporter. You must look at your story from the paper's point of view; what makes this story important enough, interesting enough, to warrant the expense of sending a reporter?

In one sense, the information you include is similar to the information in a news release: a news lead must contain the *Who, What, Where, When, Why and How* that are basic to your story. Be sure to include:

- how your event benefits your community;
- if it is sponsored by a nonprofit group;
- if proceeds are going to a serious cause;
- if a speech or a speaker should be covered, and why.

Your news lead must motivate coverage in no more than a page of writing, although you may send along a separate *fact sheet* or a *backgrounder*. A fact sheet is a chronological listing of historical or pertinent facts about your story. Like the news lead, your fact sheet should be no more than one page long. A backgrounder is a more colorful narrative history or background, no longer than two pages. Use your business stationery and begin with the same "headline" that you use for your news lead. You can supplement either a news lead or a news release with a fact sheet and a backgrounder.

Always be accurate. Editors and reporters should double-check your information, but they may not have (or take) the time, relying instead on your expertise. If the newspaper has to print a retraction because you gave incorrect information, you have lost all credibility. And, they have a very long memory.

By the way, your "headline," the phrase you use as a title for your story, *will not* be the headline used in the paper. Headlines are written by editors to fit the size and shape and tone of your story once they've decided where to put it in the paper.

Press letters, a variation on the news lead, are personal letters from you to someone you know at the newspaper selling the idea of your story. To be successful, your press letter *must* include the same information as in a news lead. You are appealing to your contact as a professional journalist, not as a personal friend.

Write a *news release* yourself when your story is straightforward, with a limited number of details. For example, use a news release when:
- you have won an award or given one to an employee;
- you're announcing an event;
- your business has hired a new administrator;
- you've moved your business;
- you've passed a milestone you want people to know about (a safety record, a financial record...)
- the story involves a major issue, but you don't want to provide more details or answer questions. This strategy may not work, of course. If the editor is on the ball, reporters will be calling anyway.

Writing in a journalistically approved format and style will help get your release printed. I hope you realize that nobody *has* to print your release just because you send it. Some people actually are surprised to learn that elementary fact!

Writing in a journalistically approved format and style will get your release printed.

Your release competes with those authorized and written by the newspaper's writer, with copy from the wire services, with syndicated columns and features the paper is paying for, and with a truly enormous stack received every day from other people who believe they, like you, have an important story that should be printed.

An editor of a small metropolitan daily paper told me she receives 200-300 unsolicited news releases *every day*. Of these, five (at the most!) will be printed. She...and other editors...chose releases that are professionally presented and are, in their judgement, newsworthy.

You have to pass that stern test...every time. If you flunk the "newsworthy" test three or four times in a row, the editor is quite likely to toss your release in the wastebasket, unopened and unread. Don't take the chance.

Some public relations experts advise faxing your release; it was good advice when fax machines were a brand new technology. Now, many organizations are clogging newsroom fax machines with news releases. Don't add to the clog; call the editor and check if your release is urgent enough...and desired strongly enough...to be faxed.

If you want your story distributed regionally or nationally, you have an alternative to mailing the release yourself. *News release wire services* charge a fee to deliver your release wherever you stipulate. A list of some of these companies is at the end of Chapter Four.

Don't confuse these companies with *wire services*, such as Associated Press (AP), United Press International (UPI) or Reuters. Wire services are electronic news delivery systems paid for by the newspapers or broadcast stations themselves.

You don't need to send your release to a wire service. If your story deserves wider attention, *news editors* will send it to AP, etc. However, decisions to send the story out for wider distribution are usually reserved for copy professionally written by the reporters.

Writing Style for Releases

A clear, concise, factual, down-to-earth writing style works best. Write what readers must know to understand your story...be complete, but then stop. Don't get fancy; don't get verbose; don't use jargon; don't use acronyms (if you do, spell out the acronym at its first use); don't make statements you can't prove.

Stay away from the drama. If your story demands drama, send a news lead and let the professional writers take over. Human interest stories are best written by a professional.

Stick with the facts in your news release. For example, "this is the *best* product," is your opinion, probably unprovable. So, state it as a quote from the president of your company, not as a fact. Instead of saying, "She's a *world-renowned* expert on...," directly quote one of your meeting's sponsors. Or better yet, leave it unsaid.

Stay away from adjectives like "exciting," "wonderful," or "amazing." What makes "it" exciting or wonderful or amazing? Forget the superlatives "best," "most," "largest," "oldest" unless you can prove what you're claiming.

When you edit your copy...and you *must* edit several times...take out most of the adjectives and the adverbs. Use the present tense and the active voice. Always use correct grammar. If you plan to write frequently, buy a copy of the latest revision of Strunk & White's The Elements of Style. For my money, it's still the best brief book on good writing that exists.

Be prepared to get a call from reporters. They may want to write your story in a different format. Assign one person at your business to take any media calls so all media get the same information.

Photographs:
To Send, or Not To Send

Don't send photographs with a news lead since you expect the newspaper to cover your story. They will use their own professional staff photographers. However, you should have photos available:
- if you have historic photos that would otherwise be unavailable to the press;
- when you send follow-up stories about an event to press representatives who were not there;
- if you're announcing an award, a promotion or some other non-feature story involving your employees;
- if the magazine editor wants supporting photos.

With the possible exception of historic shots (where choices are obviously limited), all photographs *must* be professional quality. No fuzzy, out-of-focus, grainy pictures allowed. No candid, Polaroid™shots of the award winner in the far distance.

And please, no "grip and grin" shots of the winner and award presenter shaking hands and smiling. This picture is such a cliche, no paper will run it (unless the presenter is President Clinton, of course). Well, maybe in the Sports section with Michael Jordan presenting. You get the idea.

If your photograph includes more than one person, make sure the people are spaced tightly together. Newspaper columns are not wide enough; dead space between people simply means your photo won't be used.

Another cliche photo rarely used is the speaker behind the podium. Instead, simply send a *mug shot* of the speaker (or the award winner or the person being promoted). A mug shot is so named because it's a head-and-shoulders photo in a standard size (2¼ x 3¼-inches). A standard size for other types of photographs is 5 x 7 inches, but check with the editor about their preferred size.

If you don't have an expert photographer on your staff, subcontract with one for the occasion. Here's where your Rolodex™file of freelance talent comes in handy.

Although newspapers are using more color photographs today, they are exclusively professional news and travel photos. Shoot your photos in black and white film; it's available from photography stores.

Pictures for articles written for magazines may be the exception; ask the editors if they want color photos. If so, they usually want slides.

Always identify your photos; they may get separated from the accompanying story. Type the person's name (correctly spelled, of course) on a stick-on label and attach directly to the back of the mug shot. Also send a caption further identifying the person by title, company, etc.

Historic and other kinds of photographs will need more detailed captions. Attach the caption with tape to the back of the photo. Always identify each person in the photo by position, starting from the left. Keep captions short, no longer than a paragraph, double-spaced.

The Real World

When I was an editor, once a year I received a large envelope with a news release from the national Watermelon Promotion Board after their board meeting. I recognized the envelope by the logo, a colorful wedge of red watermelon, green rind and black seeds.

That logo was the only colorful part of the 17-page release (admittedly, one year it was only 15 pages) telling all about the myriad of resolutions passed, research examined, new developments in the watermelon field (sorry), and appointments to the board.

The appointments took up most of the release, with at least one page devoted to the previous accomplishments of each new board members.

The first year I received this release, a new appointee was from the local university, for which I was working. I summarized this "newsworthy" fact into a two-paragraph release and sent it off. As I remember, even this summary was too long for the local papers, and the release was cut down to three lines.

Moral: Fire any public relations agency that charges you for producing news releases by the pound, not the page.

Broadcast Media

Tools of the Trade

Radio

Radio can be a useful tool when you're looking for publicity. It's a relatively inexpensive medium to use, and it reaches many target audiences. However, don't use radio exclusively to deliver your message, particularly if you're trying to get people to remember specifics, such as a date or a time. Everyone listens to radio while they're doing something else...driving to work, making dinner, diapering a baby, etc. Besides, who has a pencil handy when it's needed, anyway?

An article in the August 1993 <u>Public Relations Journal</u> said:

"Radio has been around for what seems like forever. But its popularity as a public relations placement tool seems just now to be heading toward the top of the charts. More and more organizations, including corporate giants...are regularly using radio to target audiences with specific messages.

"Why not? The placement opportunities are endless. There are thousands of stations. It's a relatively cheap medium. Newsrooms resemble ghost towns due to layoffs. and the dozens of radio formats make it easier to target niche audiences. "

All right, I've convinced you. How should you access radio?

■ Send a *news lead* (the same one you prepared for print media) and hope the news director has time to get back to you. Contacts will be by phone; very few stations have enough staff to pursue news interviews away from their offices.

■ Write a *radio script* for the announcer to read over the air. Write your script in an easy-to-read format. I'll tell you more about script writing later; it's not as simple as it sounds. Remember: you're writing for the ear, not the eye. Time your script by reading aloud; be sure it takes no longer than 30 seconds; 15-seconds would be even better.

If your script is intended for broadcast during the news, you can use the standard news format, if you pay careful attention to the fact that it will be read out loud. If disc jockeys are supposed to read your script during a music program, they will undoubtedly change it to fit their own personal verbal style. If you're not sure about writing a script, get a professional to help you.

National distribution (and in-house preparation) of a radio script package runs about $3,000. Several companies offer this service; some are listed at the end of Chapter Four. The cost for local distribution is obviously much less; or, you can write the script and distribute it yourself.

- A *Public Service Announcement (PSA)* is a different kettle of fish. PSAs are messages aired by the station at no cost and aimed at the public good. "Don't use drugs;" "Take a bite out of crime" (the McGruff series); Smokey the Bear's "Only you can prevent a forest fire;" are examples. You can use a PSA to educate the public about issues important to your industry (build a fence around your pool to protect toddlers, for example), but you cannot use your business name, except as a sponsor. Radio stations often will announce, "The preceding message was brought to you by....."

PSAs are often repeated several times a day or week as long as they are timely, so a *KILL DATE* needs to be on your script to tell the station's Public Affairs Director when to toss the PSA. By the way, that director is the person to contact about your PSA...either to produce it or to air it.

You can script a PSA and send it to the station <u>or</u> produce an audio tape <u>or</u> ask the station to produce it for you. Your script will be read just as it is, without music or sound effects. If you believe your PSA will be more convincing with such special effects, do it (or have it produced for you) on audio tape.

The law changed a few years ago; radio (and television) are no longer *required* to set aside a certain number of minutes to broadcast PSAs. Broadcasters continue to do so because they, too, want a good public image.

▪ Send a professionally recorded audio news release (ANR) with your news to appropriate stations (those who reach *your* particular target audience). Your message, the voice and the recording quality must all be accurately aimed at the listening audience. Of course, before sending a tape anywhere, check whether a station is interested. The production and distribution (nationally) of an audio news release package starts about $2,750. Divide that figure by approximately 10 for a local package.

▪ Appear on a radio talk show; talk show producers are often looking (sometimes desperately) for guests. They particularly like controversial guests who will arouse great interest. Does that describe you? You may be able to arrange a call-in interview, broadcast "live" or taped for later broadcast. A "call-in" interview is exactly what it sounds like -- you are interviewed over the phone by the talk show host.

▪ *Radio media tours* are a new format being used successfully for statewide, regional or national exposure. It is a series of pre-planned telephone interviews between you (or your spokesperson) and a successive group of radio stations. During the syringe tampering scare in June (1993), for example, Pepsi-Cola jammed the radio airwaves with an audio news release (ANR) chock full of reassuring sound bites from its chief executive.

Here's a short checklist to keep in mind if you want to plan a series of radio interviews over the telephone. It's taken from "The Official Radio Tour Handbook" published by North America Network, Inc. (Information in brackets are my additions):

▪ Prepare a light but informative media kit, including press releases, brochures, backgrounders. [Send to the targeted radio stations one week before calling to schedule the interview.

If you are using spokespersons, make certain they are thoroughly informed about your message.]

- Draft 8 to 10 suggested interview questions to help guide the interviewer.

- Suggest information that may be pertinent to particular cities. [This information is for use by your spokesperson.]

- Select a date and a reschedule date [with the stations]. Try to coordinate your spokesperson's schedule for morning interviews, the best time for radio interviews.

- Interviews can be tiring so you might want to spread a large tour over two or more days.

- Set aside some time before the interviews for a "prep session."

Television

Getting publicity on broadcast television demands more professional help than working with any other medium. Essentially, you have the same range of publicity choices on television as you do on radio, but getting on television may be more difficult.

- Fewer channels are available.

- The limited number of newscasts all have tremendous demands on available time.

- Most talk shows are scheduled for "dead" time. For example, they're on Sunday mornings when fewer people are listening.

■ You must depend on the channel's cameras and other commercial production facilities because the technology needed for broadcast production values is quite expensive. Buying TV studio equipment costs well over $1 million for a small facility.

Camcorders won't do unless you videotape a crime or disaster scene. The Rodney King beating in California is the best example I can think of, but this is far afield from getting publicity for your business.

■ If you want to have *video news releases (VNR)* or PSAs produced for areawide distribution, you will have to pay production houses to do them for you. That means spending money, usually several hundred dollars an hour.

Television spots take time to produce...more time than you probably imagine even if you have the best professionals to work with you. Having said that, I admit that newscasts take the least production time, with the possible exception of live talk shows.

News broadcasters work on tight deadlines, producing three (or four) half-hour broadcasts every day. They don't have the luxury of spending hours in careful post-production editing.

If you want your publicity on the nightly newscast, design the idea so your entire story can be covered in *90 seconds*. Yes, I said 90 seconds...at the maximum. A typical news story script includes a 10-second introduction by the news anchor, 15 or 20 seconds of explanation from the reporter covering your story, 45-50 seconds of "live" footage of your event, and the remainder is a closer from the reporter. Impossible to convey your idea in that short a time? Then work on it.

Working on your idea, figuring out ways to convey your image in a short time, is the hardest part of television publicity. Remember, your story has to be dramatic, visual, and at the same time, of great interest to the audience you're trying to influence.

Take just as much preparation time if you're appearing on a local talk show. You won't be working from a script, but you must carefully think through your answers to any (and all) possible questions. Most local talk show hosts want you to be comfortable. Their producers will talk to you ahead of time; have your media kit prepared and include a list of suggested questions.

Is the show's audience is large enough, or important enough to you to justify the expense of preparing a video segment? Most local talk show budgets won't cover the expense. Talk with the producer about your idea; certainly you must have his or her go-ahead before going any further. Perhaps the channel will allow you to use their camera crew and post-production editing studio at a reduced cost. If not, check into the cost of subcontracting with a production company.

Most medium- to large-market television areas have a PBS channel, often associated with your university. Check with the manager about talk and news shows. Access may be even more limited than to commercial stations because the channel management is often less concerned about local businesses. Tailor your publicity idea to their requirements. Remember, most PBS channels have smaller audiences, albeit more faithful, than are claimed by commercial channels.

If you have an idea that deserves television publicity, go to it. First, talk to the professional assignment and public affairs directors plus talk show producers at the stations. Your next alternative is going to an independent TV production house and work with their producers to put together a videotape for you to market to the stations.

Remember, TV needs dramatic, visual, exciting ideas. It's publicity with a twist.

The Real World

This particular year, the National Chicken Cooking Contest was held in Salisbury, Maryland. This was back in the days when the contest was still primarily sponsored by the Delmarva Poultry Industry. I was "loaned" from the University of Delaware to work with the public relations firm and DPI.

Conway Twitty and Loretta Lynn, the country music stars who weren't yet legends, were doing a concert in Salisbury. We were thrilled when they agreed to be interviewed by the media about how much they loved chicken. As I remember, no money changed hands. It was publicity for them and the contest.

I brought a Colonel Sanders Kentucky Fried Chicken® drumstick in a discrete brown paper sack...no use spreading the publicity around any more than necessary, right? The TV cameras caught Conway and Loretta nibbling daintily together on the same drumstick.

It made the evening TV news and the front page of the local daily paper.

Moral: In search of publicity, PR folks have been known to stretch a point.

Handling Interviews

Heaven or Hell?

Actually, an interview with a reporter should be an exercise in cooperation. Reporters are interested in getting the most accurate, best possible story out of any situation. Unless you're engaged in "damage control," trying to control unfavorable news, your aim is exactly the same.

I've written earlier about some of the problems that could get in your way; timing, location, contacting the right person, etc. It's up to you to manage your interview to get the best media exposure you possibly can.

The interview problems I'm going to write about in this chapter are primarily those you'll run into when reporters are digging for news, not necessarily good news, about your business. All your contacts with the media are not going to be confrontational.

Keep in mind the difference in your response between these two situations:
- you initiated the contact with the media, or
- they called you.

If a reporter calls you, find out who you're talking to (get their phone number and how to spell his/her name in case you need to call back) and what paper or station wants a story. What information is wanted? At that point, you decide about going ahead.

Don't panic, don't guess, don't speculate and when you finish, shut up.

Cooperation is a good idea, but an interview with reporters is an encounter with professionals doing their job. Never forget, an interview is not a conversation, no matter how friendly. It's a highly structured situation. Your role is to communicate as much information as possible about a particular topic, probably as quickly as possible, while keeping control of your interview.

"I'm on a deadline. This is a breaking news story, and I want your answers *now...or never*," insists the reporter. Is this your media nightmare? Such ultimatums happen, but rarely. Don't be intimidated. Tell the reporter(s) you *will* grant an interview, but you *must* have time to get information together. Then, live up to your word; call back.

More good advice: *Don't panic, don't guess, don't speculate, and when you're finished, shut up.*

Reporters always are on tight deadlines, but don't let this fact make you lose control. If you are working on a publicity angle, not damage control, your information will probably be as valid tomorrow as it is today. You *have* time to prepare. Let reporters know you respect their deadlines, but you must have time to get your facts straight. Of course, if you've done your homework preparing your publicity story, your facts, and key points, are already straight.

This leads to the most important "rule" about preparing for an interview:

- *Identify your key message...briefly.*

Know the *three* most important points you want to get across. More than three key points is usually too much information for people (your reporters and their readers or viewers) to remember or act on.

To be sure you identify the best three key points, start by writing down every possible statement you want to make about your story. Then ask yourself two questions:

- Which are absolutely vital from *your* point of view?
- Which are most important from the *reader/viewer* point of view?

Both questions are important; your key points must include both. But, as always, the interests and viewpoints of your readers...your target audience...take top priority.

Decide before your interview how you're going to answer difficult questions. If you have time to rehearse, ask a coworker to work with you. Every time you answer a question, include at least one of your three key points.

Keep your key points (in fact, *all* your prepared information) totally free of industry jargon. Reporters may misinterpret it; readers/viewers won't understand it. The purpose of your publicity will be lost. Jargon creeps insidiously into your thinking. It helps to talk to someone unfamiliar with your business; when that person's eyes start to glaze over, or they look puzzled...rephrase.

Questions don't get printed or aired; Your answers do.

If at all possible, don't try to explain a complicated story over the phone to a reporter in a hurry. You're inviting an article with errors and misquotes. Unless you're dealing with a radio reporter, insist the interview be done in person. If that's impossible, ask the reporter to read back vital points in your interview. Ask to have your name and title *spelled* back to you. Offer to send supporting material by FAX (or electronically by computer modem if that's possible) immediately. After all, that's why you've prepared a media kit.

Be pleasant. Reporters are vehicles to reach the public with your publicity or your side of an issue. Very few reporters are abrasive or confrontational; even cynical journalists work hard to get your side of any story. It's just good business for them. But, if you have the bad luck to deal with someone unpleasant, keep your cool. You have no other choice.

Be positive, not defensive, even though a reporter may phrase a question in a negative way. Don't let reporters put their misunderstandings or bias in your mouth; in other words, don't repeat their question. You don't want to risk being misdirected. Questions don't get printed or aired; your answers do.

When reporters rephrase your answers, make sure their wording is accurate. They're trying to make sure they understood. Help them. For print journalists, this is the time your painfully researched background material comes in handy. Radio and television reporters usually are in too much of a hurry to be interested.

You've prepared; you've researched. And still, you don't know the answer to a reporter's question. Or you believe the answer will be embarrassing to you. Don't panic.

Don't avoid answering any question you should logically be in a position to answer; you'll only generate mistrust and a belief that you're hiding something. This is where your preparation comes in. Put as positive a spin on your answer as you can. Sometimes you may have to smile and admit, "That's in the past, but here's what we're doing *now*."

The worst answer is, "No comment."

The *worst* answer is, "No comment." First of all, that answer leaves you wide open to the question, "What are you hiding...and why?" The article will reflect this suspicion. "No comment" motivates reporters to dig deeper. If you have a legal reason, say so. If you'll be able to answer the question later after you get more information, offer to contact reporters then. And do so.

Let's get this business of "off the record" out of the way. Simplify your life. Don't worry about being "on the record," "off the record," "for background only," "deep background," "for attribution only." When you talk to reporters, you're *on* the record. What you say *can* be used. Even if a reporter agrees to keep your name out of the story, the editor may overrule that commitment.

When you speak...from the podium or in the audience...at a public meeting, what you say *can* be used. Leave the fancy stuff alone until you get to be a bigwig in Washington, DC., and you can afford a highly paid public relations staff.

Is the question out of your field? Say so. Offer the name of an authority who might know. It's far better to be honest than inaccurate.

Is the question irrelevant? Smile; look the reporter pleasantly in the eye, and say, "That's an <u>interesting</u> question, but it's more important to consider...."

Don't let reporters lead you down a side track. Neither of you have the time. Americans are willing to go to amazing lengths to be polite. We will answer the most impertinent questions without thinking, "That is none of your business!"

Does the reporter start a question with, "Well, what if...?" Watch out; avoid answering hypothetical questions. Crystal-ball-gazing is hazardous; let the professional psychics get their headlines. And look silly.

It's a stupid, uninformed, inane, off-the-wall question? Just smile politely to acknowledge the question, and then repeat one of your key points. Say what *you* want to say. Don't get angry or emotional. Obviously, don't belittle the reporters; they control what finally appears in the media.

What should you do if you are asked a "laundry list," composed of three or four questions at the same time? Pick one and answer it -- the one that relates most closely to your key points.

Obviously, good reporters ask good, clear questions...most of the time. If you don't understand a question, say so before you both get confused. If the reporter makes a statement and waits for your reaction, simply say, "I don't understand what you want to know."

Another interview nightmare. Part of the question contains information you know is untrue. Now what do you do? *Correct* the misinformation in your answer, but *don't* repeat the question, particularly if your interview is being broadcast on radio or television. The more often people hear the mistake, the more apt they are to remember *it*, not your correction. You could answer simply with the correct information.

Watch out for humor. Leave the jokes for professional comedians. A response you intended in light, good-hearted fun may appear quite different in print or on the air. Sarcasm is even more dangerous.

On the other hand, being frozen-faced, always stiff, solemn and serious, leaves the wrong impression, too. You're human and it's alright to animate your feelings. You build empathy by being sincere, particularly when you're on-camera. Show your natural satisfaction, compassion, happiness, and even irritation. But don't fake; you're not an actor.

Reporters may ask your opinion about a competitor's new product. Or even say, "I understand XYZ is in trouble.

Any comment?" What an opportunity! You're offered the chance to talk about your competition. Admit it, your natural temptation is downgrading them. Don't do it. Instead, talk about why *you're* superior...what makes *you* unique. Three key points...remember them?

And, if it takes you a few seconds to think about exactly the best way to answer a question, don't worry about it. You're thinking...it's allowed. Unless you're doing a live radio or television broadcast, those few seconds of pause will be edited out before the segment gets on-air. A newspaper reporter is not likely to write, "She took time to think."

Of course, a short silence feels like a lifetime. That fact is sometimes used by reporters; it's one of their most effective "tricks of the trade." Good reporters listen deeply. They try by their questions and their body language to inspire you to answer clearly and fully. Have you ever seen a reporter nod encouragingly? They smile; they murmur, "Uh-huh?" They lean forward, waiting with, as the old cliche goes, "bated breath."

Don't be "listened" into saying something you didn't intend to say.

You know your interview is going to be recorded when dealing with broadcast media, so why panic when a newspaper reporter brings a tape recorder? Being taped is the best assurance that your quotes will be accurately reported. In fact, if you're particularly concerned about an interview, tape it yourself.

So far, the interview techniques I've written about apply both to print and broadcast media. Appearing on television demands a few additional pointers. It bears repeating; your television reporter or talk-show hosts want you to look good. Take any suggestions they offer; work *with* them. They know what they're doing. Ask if the TV station has a make-up artist available for you. Look in the monitor *before* the show begins to check your posture.

One word of warning. If you agree to appear on one of the national talk or news shows, all bets are off. Mike Wallace...Maury Povitch ...Geraldo...are not paid to make you look good. Get intensive television training, and even then, it may not do you any good.

Let's get back to your real world.

On television, your appearance is vital. The way you look has a great deal to do with your credibility. I'm not writing just about your physical beauty (thank goodness, for most of us). You communicate nonverbally.

■ Arrive on time if you're broadcasting from the studio. Don't put yourself and the station at a disadvantage by huffing and puffing in at the last minute.

■ Sit or stand straight, but not stiffly. Gesture naturally for emphasis. Lean forward to make your point. Be sincere, enthusiastic, natural. Combining those directions with your nervousness may seem pretty close to impossible. But, try. Practice as a speaker helps.

■ Don't jiggle; any motions will be exaggerated on camera.

■ If you're sitting down at your desk, lean slightly forward, with your back kept straight. Rest your arms on your desk, and keep your hands still by clasping them together.

- Relax, but don't slouch, if you're standing. Center yourself over your feet, keeping them about 6 - 8 inches apart, with one foot slightly ahead of the other.

- Smile pleasantly. You're not making a toothpaste commercial; you don't need to grimace. Of course, if your subject is serious, your face and demeanor need to reflect it. Try not to squint despite the bright, harsh lights.

- Wear comfortable, professional looking clothing...clean and unwrinkled, of course. You'll never make a mistake by being conservative. You want your audience to pay attention to your information, not your flashy tie or jewelry (unless that's what you're selling).

If you constantly pull your skirt down, it's too short. Sophisticated cameras can handle most colors better than they used to, but if you're in doubt about the color of your clothes, check with the producer. And by the way, it won't matter if your shoes are shined if your foot is in your mouth.

- Ask if the station's makeup person will be responsible for making you look good under the bright lights. If not, ask for suggestions.

- Look where the producer tells you to look. On a one-on-one interview, you'll be told to look at your interviewer, not the camera and *never* at the monitor after the interview starts.

- Never assume the camera is focused elsewhere (or that your microphone is turned off). You are *on* until told otherwise. In fact, no matter what kind of broadcast situation, *always assume you're being recorded* until the last piece of equipment is stowed or the studio lights are turned off. Amazing how much embarrassment this piece of advice will save you.

The Setting

You've read about the importance of setting the scene for a press conference. It's just as true for a standard print-media interview, and vital for a television interview.

First impressions count. Surroundings speak, even if you're not being photographed or on camera.

What's appropriate? Take down the girlie calendar; yes, I know, it shouldn't be there in the first place. Don't stage the interview in a luxuriously furnished office if you're announcing a fund-raising event. If your office is terminally messy, find another location.

Look around. See yourself and your setting as strangers will see them. What impression will you make?

The Real World

My boss was mad, sputtering, infuriated. He had just seen the news story resulting from a speech he'd given, followed by a one-on-one interview. The reporter was sharp, knowledgeable, on the agricultural beat for our local daily paper.

The quote was about research to improve cotton, a major crop in Arizona. This is a desert state concerned about water consumption, and cotton takes a goodly amount of irrigation. The story quoted my boss as using the words, "cotton, that water-sucking crop." He denied it, vehemently.

Just between you and me, I'm sure he used those exact words, even though I wasn't present at the interview. Why? The quote was too good, too telling. The reporter would never have invented it. My boss said "water-sucking crop" because he hadn't taken time to prepare for the interview as well as he'd prepared for his speech.

Unfortunately, that wasn't the end of his error. He laid down the edict, "From here on, that reporter is a non-person. Don't answer his phone calls; don't give him any interviews!"

Moral: Ego gets in the way.

Crisis!

You're a small business. You have enough trouble worrying about cash flow; you can't be bothered to plan against the remote possibility that a media firestorm could happen to you. Why should you take the time?

No matter how badly Exxon handled their public relations, the company survived the Valdez disaster in Alaska. Union Carbide coped with the Bhopal, India, explosion and survived media coverage.

You don't have their financial resources. A badly handled crisis (as far as media are concerned) can crucify you, strip you of customers and ruin your reputation. And, it may not matter how innocent you are of legal wrongdoing if the media convict you of being sleazy.

To prepare for a crisis, start by thinking through the hazards that particularly relate to your business. Do you deal, on an everyday basis, with certain hazardous chemicals? Do you dispose of regulated materials-anything from used tires to dry cleaning chemicals and a lot more? These are obvious places to begin thinking about the information you may need to give media if an accident happens.

Don't think you're off the hook if none of the above apply to you. If you handle food, you're at risk. And these days, news stories about disgruntled former employees murdering their ex-supervisors and co-workers are an almost everyday occurrence. Strikes are less common than they used to be, but picketing activists get publicity complaining about fur coats, rodeos, cosmetic testing...

You can't prevent natural disasters-damage from floods, fires, tornadoes, hurricanes-or unnatural disasters, such as a motorist driving through your front window. But you need to handle the publicity that follows.

Whether you're to blame or an innocent victim, the public will judge your business by the way you react to a crisis. And, they will form their opinions as a result of what they hear, read and watch in the media.

Plan ahead. Draft a *short* emergency action plan in advance. I recommend a short plan-no more than five pages long-because it won't work if you don't use it, practice it, update it. And, give a copy to everyone.

Who will receive *all* information about the emergency? How will receptionists and secretaries who answer the phones respond to frantic, urgent questions? Who (one person only, please) will talk to the media? Who will notify suppliers and customers (don't forget bankers, either) of a change in normal routine? Here's a very important part of your plan-who will keep your own employees up-to-date?

The head and other executives of your company are obviously heavily involved in responding to your crisis. However, don't expect them to take care of everything. For example, the responsibility for handling media should go to the most qualified person, the one most familiar with media, the most unflappable and the steadiest. One-and only one-person should be in charge of giving media interviews, planning and approving news releases, and deciding what to do in situations not covered in your five-page crisis plan.

After you've considered suggestions from everyone, write your plan in simple, straightforward English, plus whatever other languages your employees customarily use. Make sure there's a plainly labeled copy on every office desk after you've held a general meeting to explain. Update your plan every six months.

When (if) an emergency happens, be ready to respond quickly. Speed makes the difference between your complete recovery and prolonged disaster. Worry more about responding quickly-getting the word out accurately-than about the cost of damage repair. Public opinion crystallizes very fast and can be extremely difficult to change. If you delay informing the public about a health or safety problem, they won't forget.

A few words of advice from a lot of seasoned public relation's pros: *Don't try to cover up a major crisis; it won't work.* If the reporters don't call you, you need to get in touch with them. You'll never have a better opportunity to influence the effects of a crisis or an emergency than you will that first day.

Spill your guts. Tell all-within limits. Your lawyer will try to insist on far broader limits than a public relation's consultant would advise.

First limitation. If your crisis involves fatalities, give reporters the number of people killed or badly hurt-*don't release names*. Next-of-kin should not learn about such deaths through the media. Actually, police and/or hospitals will take care of releasing names. Of course, if the victims were your employees, your "crisis" responsibilities go beyond reserving the release of names; you may need to protect the victim families from exposure to reporters.

Don't speculate about the cause of a disaster such as an explosion, fire, contaminated food, etc. Give reporters all the details you can, and promise to keep them updated. Then, keep your promise.

Don't speculate about the dollar value of your loss, the length of time your business will be closed. Again, as soon as you have accurate information, update the media. Reporters understand that you won't know all the details immediately, and they respect your attempts to be accurate.

An accident or other emergency-whatever the cause-obviously won't generate good publicity. But don't be naive. Ignoring the media, stonewalling, will only cause reporters to dig and keep digging. Every day you'll see another story with another rehash of the original crisis. Your bad publicity will continue, day after day, probably with information and speculation from uninformed and inaccurate sources. Also, your employees will be pestered frequently, which will not improve their morale.

How many reporters you have to deal with depends on the nature of your crisis and on your location. A business emergency in a small town will likely attract attention only from local radio stations and newspapers-unless a large number of people are affected or endangered-or unless the nature of your crisis is so unusual that it attracts wider attention.

If you can't deal with the reporters one at a time, hold a news conference. A true emergency is one of the few times that a news conference is a legitimate necessity. If television is involved, crews will want to be at the disaster site. Press photographers will insist on pictures taken on-site. If police or safety authorities agree, allow the intrusion, but try to schedule follow-up interviews at less dramatic locations. You may need to arrange a press pool in which a selected, limited group of journalists cover the emergency site. They must agree to share photographs, video footage and information with their colleagues. Grant off-site interviews with non-pool reporters so they can file their individual stories.

As part of your crisis preparedness plan, you may need to select outside technical experts who can explain and analyze an emergency situation in your particular industry. Choose someone with credentials reporters (and the public) will trust. At the very least, prepare a media kit with background information about your business.

This book deals with media, but handling an emergency can involve far more than media. Although your media can keep public generally informed, you may need to hold local public meetings to reassure your neighbors.

Use every method of communication at your disposal to keep all your employees totally informed. Update them every day. They will influence your recovery more heavily than any other group of people

Correcting Media Mistakes

You did your best, but the story is wrong. Now what do you do? Get your temper under control first. Swearing about the biased, inaccurate media may be comforting, but it won't do you much good.

Decide whether a response is justified, based on your realistic options. Spend your energy...time...money when and where it really matters. Who read or heard the mistake? How vital an audience are they to your business? How far has the story spread? Is this the first error the media have made about your story, or one of a series? Were all the errors in one paper or station?

The question most often neglected: *Why* do you want to make a correction? "I want everybody to respect (or trust, or like) me and my business." "I want to get my boss off my back." Unfortunately, corrections probably won't accomplish either.

Frankly, if you and your business are in the news frequently, inevitably sooner or later you'll look bad because of a mistake. And sometimes, you can parlay the mistake into a bigger, more positive story because you have leverage on the offending publication.

Do you have a legitimate complaint? How big a deal is it? Having to make corrections is embarrassing to any reporter. For the sake of good human relations, don't make a big deal of a minor error.

Your primary goal is a correction that makes a difference to you and your business, not just your ego.

Quickly analyze the error to find out if the offending media are apt to make a correction that will do you any good. Your *primary* goal is a correction that makes a difference to you and your business, not just to your ego.

What kind of error was made? Was your name spelled incorrectly...were you identified as "third from left" in a photograph, when you actually were on the far right...or was the date or location of the event you're promoting misidentified? These are errors of fact a newspaper *will* correct the next day. No argument.

When a similar error of fact occurs during a radio broadcast, call immediately. Ask for a correction on the next news broadcast, which will probably be in 30 minutes. Be prepared to have your call taped; be ready to voice your corrections over the air. You get to tell your own story.

The problem with correcting a radio story is the assumption that you *will* hear the broadcasts on all stations that carry your publicity. That's not as easy as it sounds. You can ask a radio monitoring service to let you know immediately about deviations from your script. However, few monitoring services are willing to make that commitment.

Getting corrections made on television news is always problematical, especially once the offending broadcast ends. Don't waste any time; call immediately about egregious errors of fact. The announcer may have time to make corrections at the end of the news segment.

Was the story accurate as far as it went, but it didn't tell the whole story? Would the missing facts have changed the story greatly? Do you have these facts, and are you willing to be interviewed again? This kind of "error" calls for careful, reasoned judgement on your part.

Media move from one issue to the next with lightning speed. Unless your story has continuing importance in *their* viewpoint, you won't get another story. Be prepared to show the relevance of the changes you want made. Be clear about the extent of the mistaken impression made by the first story. Help them develop another story that makes your point without their having to say, "We goofed." If you have been libeled (or slandered), talk to your lawyer.

Did the story simply leave a sour taste in your mouth? The facts were indeed facts. Your quotes were accurate. But some of the words were unfair, unflattering or derogatory. Derogatory is one thing; libelous is another. Certainly, let the reporter, and the editor, know you're dissatisfied and why. Further action depends on the particular case.

Taking further action should always reflect realities. *You* will never forget the mistake; readers and viewers *will*. Very quickly. The correction won't catch everyone who read or heard the mistake. It won't be on the same page of the newspaper. Radio listeners and television viewers have moved on to another station. Consider whether exposing new people to the old error is really profitable.

If you decide the mistake doesn't seriously affect you or your business, try to get it corrected even if not publicly. Ask the reporter to put the correction in the newspaper library, connected with the original article. Your reasoning? If a follow-up story is ever written, you don't want the original error repeated.

How much damage can the media do to you? More than you want, but less than you may imagine. Writer Jonathan Alter said of the ferocious Washington D.C. media in his Newsweek Magazine column, <u>Between the Lines</u>,

"...the media beast's very insatiability eventually provides a measure of safety for its prey. A charge must be reprinted 100 times and turned into a Jay Leno joke to have much real impact. Even then it's soon forgotten. The Japanese have a maxim: after 75 days, no one remembers."

What is true in national news is even more certain in local happenings, only more so. No one remembers a week later.

Always attack the error in the story, not the reporters as people. First contact the reporter who made the error before getting in touch with the editor. To make changes as fast as needed in radio and television, talk to the directors or producers. Then take your problem as high up the ladder as you believe warranted. Also consider whether this reporter has made errors about you in the past.

Additional Options

1. Writing a letter to the editor column is an excellent remedy because letters are widely read. Make sure your letter is as convincing as possible. Here's how:

▪ Limit your letter to a tightly-defined specific subject on one page. Explain why you object to a particular story, but don't assume your readers have read or remember it.

▪ Don't rant and rave. Write calmly, logically. If necessary, use statistics, but sparingly.

▪ Edit your letter to be absolutely positive your grammar and spelling are correct.

▪ Sign your letters; include your phone number (which won't be printed). Newspapers won't print your letter without checking that it actually came from you. You can ask that your name be withheld, but don't make the request lightly.

2. Ask to write a column placed on the *Op-Ed page* (the page opposite the editorial page) refuting the mistake by discussing the issue. Editors will use three criteria to judge your request:
   A. How well can you write?
   B. How important or newsworthy is the issue?
   C. How credible an expert are you?

3. When you strongly believe the newspaper is biased against, not only your own company, but also your industry, request a meeting with the *editorial board*. These are the people who are responsible for the paper's official policies.

In this case, you're not trying to correct a specific story or to generate news coverage. You want to provide background information the board may have been unfamiliar with. Changing editorial policies is a long-term, extremely difficult procedure; don't expect fast (or any) results.

4. Correct a mistake made on broadcast newscasts by asking to appear on a relevant talk show. This is tricky, but it sometimes works. Be sure you are well-prepared to debate with your talk show host. Don't forget, you will be exposing the issue to a different audience.

5. Buy an ad in the offending publication. You will control what it says and where it's placed. Whether it's worth the cost depends on how deeply the mistake will hurt your business. These ads are different from the usual advertising used to encourage people to buy your product or service. The ads are up front about correcting what you believe is a serious media mistake. You can quote the offending article and explain your side.

This is the approach taken by Mobil Oil Corporation when they decided the media had an anti-business (or at least, an anti-oil company) bias. They bought advertising in many of the most prestigious magazines to promote Mobil Oil's viewpoint. The ads are extremely well-written and have since been packaged as a book.

6. Take legal action? Check with your lawyer, and the state of your budget. This is not an option you should take lightly.

Mistakes *do* happen, but if you follow the instructions in this book, media misdemeanors are far less likely. Not impossible, unfortunately, but unlikely. Don't allow possible errors to discourage you from dealing with the media. You will be well repaid by the benefits.

Appendix I

MEDIA GLOSSARY

■ *Actuality:* A live audio recording taped to be played back during a radio news broadcast. The person recorded may have been on the telephone or on the news scene.

■ *Advisory:* A notice to a newsroom to alert them to an event; if the event is statewide, regional or national, the advisory usually is sent by the wire services. Advisories are very brief and not intended to be published or broadcast.

▪ *Analysis:* An examination of a news story in detail, usually written by a senior journalist, columnist or TV anchor. An example of analysis is the follow-up of presidential campaign debates. Analyses are always by-lined, and put forward a point of view.

▪ *Assignment Director:* The person in charge of sending out broadcast crews to cover a specific story. Speak to the assignment director when you have a story idea for television.

▪ *Backgrounder:* A learning session for news people, usually offered for highly complex issues. In politics, backgrounders are given by people who don't wish to be quoted directly. Very risky, they should only be organized by professional public relations experts and should not replace press conferences.

In a different use of the term, sources also can provide written *background* material to news media to help them get additional information. This background material is not considered from an anonymous source.

▪ *Beat:* A reporter's area of specialization. Reporters are often switched from one beat to another, so it does not necessarily refer to special education in the field. Usually only larger daily newspapers or network broadcast reporters have a specific beat. Reporters without special beats are called "general assignment" reporters.

▪ *Deadline:* The time by which a reporter (print or broadcast) must have a story completed.

▪ *Editor:* Larger newspapers have management positions called "city desk editor," "assignment editor" and "copy editor." All are newsroom management positions. Each beat or "desk" also may have an editor. However, senior journalists may outrank most editors and work independently.

■ *Editorial Board:* The group of appointed senior journalists who write the newspaper editorials after the paper's positions on issues has been determined by the board, managing editors and the publisher.

■ *Event:* A news conference, happening, speech, meeting, photo opportunity, etc. The event is a specific occasion for news coverage.

■ *Feature:* An interesting story, usually involving human interest, that is not highly topical or newsworthy. Not time-sensitive.

■ *Hook:* The "angle" or piece of information aimed at attracting the attention of a reporter or editor who reads your news tip or release.

■ *Human Interest:* How are real people, usually named, involved in your story? Are people overcoming odds...facing good or bad fortune...doing something unusual or even extraordinary?

■ *Lead:* The first paragraph of a news story, it determines whether people read the rest of the article.

■ *Libel:* The malpractice of journalism. Libel occurs when a person is defamed by an inaccurate news story or even a photograph.

■ *News or Press Conference:* People make themselves available for questioning at a specified time and place for reporters from a group of media outlets. A conference gets the story out to all reporters at the same time. Must be carefully planned, and a press conference should be considered only when there is a genuine news event or story.

▪ *News Release:* A statement written in journalistic format and style, used to convey news to media.

▪ *Newsroom:* The place where news is processed and prepared for print or broadcast.

▪ *Off-the-record:* Information the reporter agrees not to report, or at least, not to attribute to you. A very dangerous game, best played only in Washington D.C. political circles. A public event and the comments made there are, by their very nature, "on-the-record." You cannot ask for secrecy after making a statement. Even if reporters agree to off-the-record, the editor may overrule them.

▪ *Op-Ed Piece:* An opinion piece written by someone with a particular point of view, usually run OPposite the EDitorial page, thus the name. Papers often use outside experts (non-journalists) to write op-ed pieces.

▪ *Photo Op:* An abbreviation for photo opportunity. It appeals particularly to television reporters. An imaginative photo setup will help you get coverage.

▪ *Producer:* The TV reporter's editor who works in the field and in the studio to help put the story together. In radio, the producer runs the control board and may screen calls for a telephone talk show.

▪ *Publisher:* The person who runs a newspaper or magazine; he or she may be the owner. Every department reports to the publisher, including advertising, circulation, accounting, promotion and editorial.

■ *Wire Service:* An organization that gathers and transmits news, but does not publish or broadcast on its own. The wire service supplies news to subscribers, such as daily newspapers, radio stations and television stations. The Associate Press (AP), United Press International (UPI) and Reuters are well-known wire services, but there are many others.

■ *News Release Wire Services* Companies that will deliver your news releases (which, for a fee, they will write for you) simultaneously nationally or regionally to as many newspapers as you want. Similar companies will deliver audio tapes or video news releases to broadcast media.

MEDIA DIRECTORIES
MAILING LIST SOURCES

Bacon's Information, Inc.
332 S. Michigan Ave.
Chicago, IL   60604   (312) 922-2400
FAX (312) 922-3127

> *Publicity Checkers* lists trade and consumer print media
> *Business/Financial Directory* lists business and financial media and journalists
> *Radio/TV Directory* covers broadcast media w/ 54 cable, talk show & interview contacts
> *Media Alerts* lists editorial calendars, conventions and trade shows
> Bacon's also offers a print media clipping service.

Editor & Publisher
11 W 19th Street
New York, NY 10011   (212) 675-4380

> *Editor & Publisher International Yearbook* is a 700-page newspaper encyclopedia, listing daily and weekly newspapers in all U.S. states, Canadian provinces and many foreign countries. Wire services and syndication services are also listed.
> *Editor & Publisher International Broadcast Yearbook* offers the same complete listing for broadcast outlets, both radio and television, including cable.
> *Market Guide* is a complete directory of facts about the U.S. and Canadian newspaper markets.

Hudson's Media Directories
44 W. Market St.
Rhinebeck, NY 12572   (914) 876-2081

> *Hudson's Subscription Newsletter Directory*
> *Hudson's Washington (D.C.) Directory*

Gale Research Inc.
P.O. Box 33477
Detroit, MI 48232-5477
1-800-877-GALE   FAX (313) 961-6083

> *The Gale Directory of Publications & Broadcast Media* has 37,000 entries with information on newspapers, magazines, radio and television stations, plus cable systems.
>
> *Directories in Print* lists 14,000 national and international source books and business directories.
>
> *The Gale Directory of Newsletters* includes organizational and other newsletters found nowhere else.

Media Distribution Services (MDS)
307 West 36th Street
New York, NY 10018-3282
1-800-MDS-3282   FAX (212) 714-9092

> Sells media lists for mailing & faxing news releases. Databases have names, titles, editorial interests, phone & fax numbers of 150,000+ contacts at 40,000+ print and broadcast media in the U.S. and Canada, plus national security analysts and members of Congress and staffs.

National News Production and Distribution Services

Audio News Release Services

Media Tracks Communications
1235 Wood Ave.
Deerfield, IL 60015
Phone: (708) 317-1515   FAX: (708) 317-1570

Specializes in healthcare and food/nutrition ANR, with guaranteed placement in a minimum of 80% of the top 50 markets. They also write, produce and distribute audio PSAs.

Media Distribution

Media Distribution Services
307 West 36th Street
New York, NY 10018-6496
Phone: (800) MDS-3282   FAX: (212) 714-9092

Largest public relations media, mailing & printing service.

News USA
4601 Eisenhower Ave.
Alexandria, VA 22304
Phone: (703) 461-9500   FAX: (703) 461-9506

Editorial Publicity Distribution, placement and clippings service. Turns press releases into column, radio series, special events coverage and Hispanic media coverage. Distribution to 10,000+ newspapers and 6,000+ radio stations. National multimedia campaigns start at $4,700, including writing, printing, postage, clippings and reports.

PR Newswire
1515 Broadway, 32nd Floor
New York, NY 10036
Phone: (800) 832-5522   FAX: (212) 596-1537

Operates large facsimile communications system, transmitting corporate news to reach your list with any text or graphic information simultaneously via more than 100 dedicated lines. Can also assign an 800 number to documents or entire databases on their computers for a target audience to call and retrieve, 24-hours every day.

Business Wire
1185 Ave. of the Americas, 3rd Floor
New York, NY 10036
Phone: (800) 221-2462   FAX: (212) 575-1854

Business Wire is an electronic media relations wire service to distribute full-text news releases simultaneously to the news media and investment community worldwide.

Southwest Newswire
2301 North Akard, 3rd Floor
Dallas, TX 75201
Phone: (214) 871-2940

Simultaneously delivers time-critical news to more than 160 newsrooms in Texas, Oklahoma, Louisiana and Arkansas. Also can send news release to other U.S. regions, Canada and internationally.

Associated Release Service
2 North Riverside Plaza
Chicago, IL 60606
Phone: (312) 726-8693   FAX: (312) 726-8596

Specializes in quality reproduction and pinpoint distribution of press releases in all formats -- print, electronic, press kits, etc. -- targeted to editors and broadcasters by name, in the U.S. and Canada. Will record releases to radio and TV, the latter in slide/script format.

Empire Information Services
P.O. Box 742
Schenectady, NY 12301-0742
Phone: (518) 372-0785   FAX: (518) 372-0787

Provides customized delivery of news releases over a proprietary computer network to more than 1,500 media in New York, New Jersey, Pennsylvania and New England. National news network also available.

Photo Distribution Services

Weick Photo DataBase, Inc.
P.O. Box 58408
Dallas, TX 75229
Phone: (214) 416-3686

A computer-to-computer service makes publicity photos available to more than 1,000 U.S. and foreign newspapers and other media so they can instantly retrieve photos in a press-ready format.

Satellite Television Services

Conus Communications
3415 University Ave.
Minneapolis, MN 55414
Phone: (612) 642-4680   FAX: (612) 642-4681

Offers nationwide video and satellite services. Video news releases, satellite media tours, teleconferences, event production and transmission can be provided on a remote basis by their mobile units or at TV production and transmission facilities in Washington, DC or Minneapolis.

J-NEX Television
5455 Wilshire Blvd., Suite 2010
Los Angeles, CA 90036
Phone: (213) 934-4356

From conception to completion, J-NEX produces satellite media tours, electronic press kits, video news releases, corporate video, national media distribution, videoconferencing, and public service announcements.

Potomac Television/Communications, Inc.
500 N. Capitol Street NW
Washington DC 20001
Phone: (202) 783-8000   FAX: (202) 783-1861

Produces and distributes video news releases, satellite media tours, media training, videoconferencing, and PSAs.

Chanticleer Communications, Inc.
8760A Research Blvd., Suite 510
Austin, TX 78758
Phone: (512) 338-0095   FAX (512) 338-1862

  Specializes in video news releases, videoconferencing,
satellite media tours and corporate video.

MEDIALINK
708 Third Ave.
New York, NY 10017
Phone: (212) 682-8300   FAX: (212) 682-2370

  Distributes video public relations in the U.S., Canada
and Europe. Offices in Los Angeles, Chicago, Washington and
London. Distributes to TV newsrooms; distributes and offers
full technical coordination of satellite media tours and broadcast
live events.

On the Scene Productions, Inc.
5900 Wilshire Blvd., Suite 1400
Los Angeles, CA 90036
Phone: (213) 930-1030   FAX: (213) 930-1840

  Produces full range of electronic publicity, including
satellite media tours, video-teleconferencing, video news
releases and public service announcements. Offers one-on-one
placement with station producers.

News Lead Format

(Use Business Letterhead Stationery)

CONTACT: Your name, address and phone number
DATE:

(Leave the top ⅛ of the page blank for editor's use)

Title of Your News Lead (Make it <u>Catchy, Exciting</u>)

DATELINE (Town, State): You need to tell about your story idea in the most interesting way possible. What makes your idea newsworthy? Put it in the first sentence. Be sure to give all the information the editor needs to know to make a decision.

Indent all paragraphs. Double-space all copy. The paragraphs should be no longer than 6 lines, with no more than 4 sentences. Limit the news lead to one page, preferably with no more than 3-4 paragraphs.

-30- or, #### or, END

News Release Format

(Use business letterhead stationery)

FOR IMMEDIATE RELEASE (Or a specific release date)

CONTACT: (Name, address, phone)

Leave the top ⅙ of the page blank for editors

Title of Your Press Release

DATELINE (town, state): Your beginning sentence (the lead) should be short and to the point. Your lead is your only chance to catch your reader's and the editor's attention. Start with the most important information.

Indent all paragraphs. Double-space all copy. Keep your sentences short. Eliminate all jargon and acronyms unless your release goes only to trade magazines. Be factual and always accurate. Keep paragraphs to four lines, containing no more than three sentences. Double-check all spelling.

-MORE-

Title Page 2

For releases longer than one page (but *never* longer than two pages), center the word (MORE) at the bottom of page one. End the page at the end of a paragraph, even if you leave a wide bottom margin.

Start the next page of your news release on a separate sheet of paper with a brief title and the page number (see the beginning of this page).

At the end of your release, write and center:

-30-

or, ####

or, END

Caption Format

(Use letterhead stationery)

CONTACT: Name, Address and Phone number

DATELINE (Town, State):   Officials from XYZ Corporation are breaking ground for a new $150 million facility on Tucson's north side. They are: (left to right) John Jones, XYZ president from New York City; Mary Smith, XYZ plant manager in Tucson; and Richard Roe, the facility architect from Phoenix.

####

Photo by Susan Smith, XYZ Corporation

Radio Script Format

(Use letterhead stationery)

CONTACT: Name and office phone

FOR RELEASE: date

KILL DATE: date to discontinue using script

LENGTH: timed, in seconds

YOUR TITLE

USE 1.5 INCH MARGINS ON BOTH SIDES; DO

NOT JUSTIFY (USE A RAGGED-RIGHT MARGIN).

TRIPLE-SPACE; DO NOT HYPHENATE WORDS AT

THE END OF A LINE. YOUR STORY SHOULD <u>NOT</u> BE

LONGER THAN ONE PAGE. USE ALL CAPITAL

LETTERS.

TO AVOID CONFUSION, PUT THE PHONETIC

SPELLING IN PARENTHESES AFTER ALL NAMES

THAT ARE HARD TO PRONOUNCE.

####

PSA Script Format

Use Your Letterhead

FOR RELEASE: Monday, Nov. 8, 1993

CONTACT: Lorraine Kingdon, 555-5555

KILL DATE: November 25, 1994

LENGTH: :10 seconds

SAFE THANKSGIVING FOOD

KEEP <u>YOUR</u> TURKEY SAFE. AFTER YOUR

FEAST, PUT THE BIRD BACK INTO THE

REFRIGERATOR TO COOL -- SO YOU CAN <u>ENJOY</u>

TOMORROW'S LEFTOVERS.

####

Appendix II

Bibliography

Biagi, Shirley.: *Media/Impact: An Introduction to Mass Media*, Updated First Edition, Wadsworth Publishing Company, Belmont, California, 1990.

Baker, Kim and Sunny Baker.: *How to Promote, Publicize, and Advertise Your Growing Business: Getting the Word Out Without Spending a Fortune,* John Wiley & Sons, Inc., New York, 1992.

Doty, Dorothy I.: *Publicity and Public Relations,* Barron's Educational Series, Inc., New York, 1990.

Fletcher, Tana and Julia Rockler.: *Getting Publicity: A Do-It-Yourself Guide for Small Business and Non-Profit Groups,* International Self-Counsel Press Ltd., Vancouver, British Columbia, Canada, 1991.

Irvine, Robert B.: *When You Are the Headline: Managing a Major News Story,* Dow-Jones Irwin, Homewood, Illinois, 1987.

Meyers, Gerald C.: *When It Hits the Fan: Managing the Nine Crises of Business,* New american Library, Bergenfield, New Jersey, 1987.

Ramacitti, David F.: *Do-It-Yourself Publicity,* American Management Association, New York, 1991.

Rosengarten, Ian B.: *How to Market Your Business: An Introduction to Tools and Tactics for Marketing Your Business,* Sourcebooks, Inc., Naperville, Illinois, 1993.

Shiller, Ed.: *Managing the Media,* Bedford House Publishing Corporation, Toronto, Ontario, Canada, 1989.

Patrick, Colleen.: *Mind Over Media: Everybody's Untimate Authority on Media Access from an Insider's Point of View,* Comprehensive Health Education Foundation, Seattle, Washington, 1987.

Walker, Morton.: *Advertising and Promoting the Professional Practice,* Hawthorn Books, Inc., New York, 1979.

Wood, Robert J.: *Confessions of a PR Man,* New American Library, New York, 1988.

Index